fundamental Catholic teaching, replies to the objections, and then cites resources for further study. This format makes for an excellent and quick resource for Catholics—clergy and laity alike. Think of it like a playbook that helps advance the ball in conversations about the faith. In a time where brevity and coming quickly to the point are appreciated and often very necessary, this book is a most valuable resource. Buy a copy and keep it near at hand!"

MSGR. CHARLES POPE
Pastor of Holy Comforter-St. Cyprian Parish, Washington, D.C.

"A very reliable and clear guide to some very important questions. This book makes an important contribution to resolving the confusion about truth that has so weakened the lives of so many Catholics."

RALPH MARTIN S.T.D.
Director of Graduate Theology Programs in the New Evangelization,
Sacred Heart Major Seminary

"With the heart of a spiritual father and the wisdom of a seasoned seminary formator, Fr. Carter Griffin offers clear, insightful explanations that reveal the intelligibility of the Catholic faith. Spiritual seekers looking for the inner reasonableness, goodness, and beauty of faith will find in these pages wisdom offered with the courage and charity of a contemporary Christian apologist."

JEM SULLIVAN
Author of *Believe, Celebrate, Live, Pray:*
A Weekly Guide to the Catechism of the Catholic Church

CROSS-EXAMINED

CROSS-EXAMINED

Catholic Responses to the World's Questions

FR. CARTER GRIFFIN

EMMAUS ROAD PUBLISHING

Steubenville, Ohio
www.emmausroad.org

Emmaus Road Publishing
1468 Parkview Circle
Steubenville, Ohio 43952

Library of Congress Control Number: 2021939304
ISBN: 978-1-64585-142-4 Paperback | 978-1-64585-143-1 Ebook

Cover design and layout by Emily Demary
Cover image: *Glory of Resurected Jesus* by Guido Reni (1575 - 1642),
Duomo di Milano, Milan, Italy. Photo by Renáta Sedmáková.

To Our Lady, the Queen of Apostles

Preach the word, be urgent in season and out of season, convince, rebuke, and exhort, be unfailing in patience and in teaching.

For the time is coming when people will not endure sound teaching, but having itching ears they will accumulate for themselves teachers to suit their own likings, and will turn away from listening to the truth and wander into myths.

As for you, always be steady, endure suffering, do the work of an evangelist, fulfil your ministry.

2 Timothy 4:2–5

TABLE OF CONTENTS

INTRODUCTION

"Always be prepared to make a defense to any one who calls you to account for the hope that is in you, yet do it with gentleness and reverence."
—1 Peter 3:15

Like many others, my journey to the Catholic faith was made possible by Catholics who were ready to explain the reasonability of our faith and who were prepared, as St. Peter enjoined, "to account for the hope" that is in us. Though my conversion took place over twenty-five years ago, I find that same hunger for a reasoned exposition of the faith—that is, "apologetics"—to be undiminished today.

For the past ten years I have been engaged in the formation of seminarians for the Catholic priesthood. As part of their training, I prepared some outlines to explore various "hot button" issues from a Catholic point of view. Over time, these explorations coalesced into a two-year cycle of topics that was progressively refined by the questions, insights, and critiques from seminarians. Several of them suggested that publishing these notes could benefit a wider audience. Hence the book you hold in your hands.

My goal was modest: to marshal, on two sides of a single sheet of paper, a concise summary of Catholic teaching on a particular topic, together with its principal objections and possible responses to those objections. In this way, loosely following an ancient method of argumentation, seminarians would not only gain a grasp of the key ideas in controversial teachings, but also glimpse the typical (and often compelling) objections to those teachings and how a Catholic might respond.

In my discussions with seminarians, I found that reviewing the objections to Church teaching was often the most valuable part of our conversation. We live in a shrill and impatient age, and respectfully considering the viewpoint of those who disagree with us does not come naturally. It is a useful exercise for us all. In a culture where many talk and few listen, listening is perhaps the most important skill that an apostolic Christian must develop. Binx Bolling says in Walker Percy's *The Moviegoer*, "I have discovered that most people have no one to talk to, no one, that is, who really wants to listen. When it does at last dawn on a man that you really want to hear about his business, the look that comes over his face is something to see."[1]

It is my hope that these short dialogues will not be perceived as pat answers intended to close conversations but rather as opportunities to spark a deeper and more interesting exchange of ideas.

Apologetics comes from a Greek word meaning "defense," usually a legal defense or a reasoned defense of one's position. It is by nature an abridged exposition of the faith—especially when explosive topics are distilled into twelve hundred to fourteen hundred words. Having a grasp of apologetics is not the same thing as having a grasp of the full beauty of Catholic teaching. I insist on this when introducing the material to our seminarians and repeat it often during our apologetics workshops. In these synopses, weighty thoughts are sometimes compressed into a single phrase, objections that deserve much more attention are summarized in one or two sentences, and nuances in Catholic doctrine can be lost. Such was the price of condensing the matter into so small a space.

On the other hand, there is something valuable about identifying the very core of a topic and its most persuasive objections. It is a snapshot, so to speak, of the various sides of a tricky dogmatic or moral issue. These snapshots are like photographs of the Alps above the cloudline. You see only the peaks, but you behold them in all their magnificence. It is true that a snapshot will never convey the intricate detail observed by a hiker, but it is a breathtaking view—and offers a perspective, and occasionally insights, that a hiker will miss.

These snapshots, then, do not replace a more penetrating analysis of each topic and certainly do not convey the human sympathy and winsomeness meant to be used in actual conversations. Still, they offer a panorama that can easily be lost in closer studies of these contentious issues. In that sense, I believe this approach complements more traditional apologetic and catechetical resources. In their very brevity they invite wider discussion.

---

[1]   Walker Percy, *The Moviegoer* (New York: Alfred A. Knopf, 1960), 64.

Why study apologetics at all? There are at least three principal reasons.

First, because we believe that the Catholic faith is true, and everyone has a right to hear the truth. In his or her baptism every Catholic receives a personal, apostolic commission from the Lord to help others embrace that truth. As St. Paul wrote, "Necessity is laid upon me. Woe to me if I do not preach the Gospel!" (1 Cor 9:16). For St. Paul, and for us, this is not a mere obligation. The more convinced we are by the truth, beauty, and goodness of the Gospel—the full Gospel proclaimed in the Catholic Church—the more earnestly we desire others to receive it. The study of apologetics can help us to articulate the faith in such a way that others, whether non-Catholics or fallen-away Catholics, are more likely to grasp it, appreciate its truth and splendor, and ultimately embrace it.

Reasoned thought about Catholic doctrine does not remove all difficulties. Many teachings, after all, we know only from revelation and cannot be apprehended through reason alone. Even in these cases, however, apologetics can demonstrate that the teaching is never against reason or irrational, even when it is "above" reason, or super-rational. We can show that embracing the faith will never require anyone to do violence to his or her reason. On the contrary, a candid acknowledgement of perceived difficulties and opposing arguments shows a confidence in the truth of Catholic teaching and a willingness to engage any and all well-disposed interlocutors.

Second, we study apologetics because there are many prejudices and misunderstandings about the Catholic faith which impede others from accepting it. As Venerable Fulton Sheen once wrote, "There are not over a hundred people in the United States who hate the Catholic Church. There are millions, however, who hate what they wrongly believe to be the Catholic Church . . . . As a matter of fact, if we Catholics believed all of the untruths and lies which were said against the Church, we probably would hate the Church a thousand times more than they do."[2]

One person believes that the Church discriminates unjustly against women by forbidding their priestly ordination. Another that the Church requires the elderly and sick to be kept alive for as long as

---

[2] Fulton J. Sheen, preface to *Radio Replies*, by Leslie Rumble and Charles Mortimer Carty (Charlotte, NC: Tan Books, 1979)

possible with every medical procedure available, regardless of pain or expense. Another that each word that a pope utters or writes is to be accepted as infallible by Catholics. These are simply mistakes, but very common ones—and difficult to dislodge. Apologetics can help overcome these stubborn preconceptions which pose false obstacles to conversion.

Third, apologetics increases the Catholic's own confidence and love for his or her faith. Reasoned argumentation can help us appreciate the beauty of our religion, the scriptural and rational roots of its doctrine, the proportion and balance and interplay among its various teachings. Perhaps even more importantly, apologetics can help us understand and respect the arguments made against our faith, giving us a wider vision and more generous approach to those who disagree with us. Our intellectual opponents are not personal enemies. The vast majority are not malicious or slow-witted. At the same time, their arguments against Catholic doctrine are not unanswerable. It is true that sometimes in a conversation, we do not know to respond. Sometimes, in fact, our best answer will be, "I don't know, but I'll find out!" It is apologetics that gives us that confidence because we know that we *will* find out. We are certain that someone, somewhere, has deeply considered the objection already and addressed it calmly and thoroughly.

It should be cautioned that apologetics is an intellectual instrument that, like any instrument, can be used or misused. The goal of these dialogues is not to vanquish an opponent in a debate. If we wield apologetics like a club, we will probably find ourselves welcoming very few friends into full communion with the Catholic Church. And we may well find ourselves falling deeper and deeper into the sinkhole of spiritual pride.

St. Peter said that we should "be prepared to make a defense to anyone who calls you to account for the hope that is in you," and then he added, "*yet do it with gentleness and reverence.*" Our explanations of the faith must be done calmly, rationally, and charitably. That is how we show reverence both for the doctrines themselves and for the sacred ground that is the human soul. Zeal for the faith is admirable and must be fostered, today more than ever, but how tragic it would be if the outburst of our own zeal became the very obstacle for another soul in its encounter with the Lord.

Our Blessed Lord called himself "the Way, and the Truth, and the Life" (John 14:6). It seems to me that this is not simply a listing of three characteristics but rather an itinerary in itself. The "way" of discipleship reaches eternal "life" because each touches the "truth" of the Gospel. May these pages contribute to a deeper love for the faith we hold dear, a firmer desire for others to embrace it, and a greater boldness to speak about our beloved Jesus and his life-giving doctrine so that more and more souls may walk on the way of truth towards the joy of eternal life.

Fr. Carter Griffin
Washington, D.C.

NOTES ON
THE CONTENT

The topics contained in this book are some of the more controversial issues that Catholics face in typical conversations today, both with other Christians and with those of a more secular outlook. It is not intended to be a comprehensive course in apologetics, still less in theology. There is no attempt, for instance, to propose a systematic defense of the Catholic faith in response to other religions or even to cover all the major topics that separate us from other Christian communions.

In every case but one, the objections, Catholic teaching, and responses are in answer to a specific question which is identified at the top of each section. The one exception is in the matter of capital punishment, which in light of a recent change to the Catechism, is presented as a prudential defense of both sides of the question. Since the Catechism change cannot be intended as a radical break from the ancient teaching of the Church and the Scriptures, the matter is addressed accordingly.

Some readers may be disappointed that certain questions are not addressed. In truth, I myself found it difficult to decide which topics to cover. Many of the decisions were dictated by the format of these dialogues. For instance, topics that are too historical—such as the Old Testament "genocides," the Inquisitions, or the Crusades— simply do not lend themselves easily to this tight objection-and-response approach. The same is true of thorny historical issues such as the Church's uneven, though on the whole creditable, response to slavery. Other topics I considered too complex, nuanced, or prudential in nature to cover in this format, for example, social justice questions like that of racism, a living wage, immigration concerns, environmental stewardship, or the suitability of Catholics attending non-Catholic weddings. All are important topics but not right for this book.

While the book may be read straight through or used as a reference work, the reader should keep in mind that these questions were originally discussed in a group setting, taking each point in turn. Readers may find the material to be most accessible and engaging when they talk it over with others.

Sources

The primary sources for these arguments are the Bible (the text is from the *Revised Standard Version*, Second Catholic Edition), the *Catechism of the Catholic Church* (noted as "CCC"), and the documents of the Second Vatican Council. I cite sources when I quote a document or an author, but in an effort to keep the text more readable I do not cite general references to authors or other matters that can be easily looked up. There is a selection of "further study" at the end of each question if the reader wishes to engage in additional research.

GOD AND ETERNITY

EXISTENCE OF GOD

How can we know that God exists?

Objection 1
The fact that we are even asking whether God exists implies that God does not exist. If God existed, there would be ample and undeniable evidence of it.

Objection 2
Throughout history, "God" was the explanation given for inexplicable phenomena. Modern science has undermined the need for the all-inclusive myth of God.

Objection 3
If God is infinite and we are finite, it would be impossible to reach or even comprehend God. Thus, even if God exists, it would be irrelevant to our day-to-day lives. The question of God's existence, then, is moot.

Objection 4
God, assuming he is omnipotent and good, cannot exist because he would not allow the suffering and evil that we experience in the world.

Objection 5
The Christian claim that God became man, was crucified, died, was buried, and then rose again from the dead is totally unreasonable and only further discredits the childish fantasy of God.

CATHOLIC TEACHING

+ **The desire for God is written into the human heart.** In every human soul is the desire and longing for God, the profound conviction that the things of this world do not ultimately satisfy us. Though contemporary secular culture often blunts this desire, history testifies to this longing through the various expressions given by cultures to the question of our origins and our destiny. As hunger is evidence that food exists, our desire for the eternal is evidence that God exists.

+ **We can know God through reason.** One proof for the existence of God argues that all things change and are moved by another. This series, however, must be initiated by an "unmoved mover" who is outside the chain of cause and effect, one who sets it all in motion. This unmoved mover is God, who is the transcendent cause of everything. Another demonstration for God's existence is the argument from design: the intelligible order and beauty of the universe strongly suggest an intelligent and wise Being who designed it.

+ **God is the foundation of the moral life.** Some thinkers such as St. John Henry Newman have approached the question of God's existence from a different point of view. Conscience, they argue, as the inner judgment of moral right and wrong, is itself a powerful argument for the existence of God. Without a Being who is the source of truth and goodness, it is difficult to identify the objective basis for virtue and vice in human lives. In addition, the Final Judgment implies an ultimate accountability for all our thoughts and actions and the assurance that injustice will, in the end, be righted. Most people, atheists included, want to live a moral life, want others to do so, and want justice to be done. Those desires are evidence that God exists.

+ **In the Incarnation of Jesus Christ, our loving God condescended to assume a human nature and so bring us within reach of himself.** He walked among us, suffered with us, and experienced everything we experience (except for sin)—including death. God became man to demonstrate his love, to give us a model of holiness, and to help us become like him. By uniting divine nature and human nature in one person, God invites us into intimate communion with him. Above all, **since we cannot**

bring about our own forgiveness, the Incarnation means that God has himself entered into the disorder of sinful humanity to reunite us to God. In complete solidarity with us, God freely chose to enter into the fullness of human experience. By dying on the Cross and being raised on the third day, God overcame even the power of death, opening for us the gates of heaven.

REPLY

Reply to Objection 1: If he existed, God would reveal himself more clearly. This objection does not account for the natural ways God *has* revealed himself to us, as sketched above, though we may often fail to perceive him. More importantly, the objection does not acknowledge the importance of faith in our relationship with God. Faith is a gift from God that makes it possible to know and love him. It is a way of knowing, distinct but not opposed to reason. It opens a wider space for freedom so that we can embrace God in a fully human way. God will never force his love upon us.

Reply to Objection 2: Modern science has superseded belief in God. Science, despite its many achievements and understanding of natural phenomena, still cannot answer the deepest questions of all, such as: *Where does the universe come from? How do I distinguish good and evil? What happens to me after death?* Scientists sometimes try to answer these questions, but science ceases to be science when it makes pronouncements about matters outside its field of competence. Often, the notion that science has superseded God is based on the idea that God is simply the "biggest thing" out there. But this is not correct; God is not one being among many. God is Being itself, the One who sustains all in being, who causes all that is. While science cannot address these questions, it can discover evidence that points to the reality of God. In this capacity, the findings of recent centuries have invariably corroborated the tenets of religious belief.

Reply to Objection 3: An infinite God is irrelevant to finite human beings. It is true that God is infinite and completely transcends creation, including humanity. But this objection fails to account for the possibility that an omnipotent and loving God could himself bridge the gap between his infinite nature and our finite nature, which is precisely the Christian claim of the Incarnation. God is not a Deity who merely "winds the clock" of creation and has nothing to do with our lives.

God has entered history and time to live among us.

Reply to Objection 4: Death and suffering disprove the existence of a good God.
The problem of evil is a real one, and it challenges all believers. Nevertheless, evil does not disprove the existence of a good and all-powerful God. To use an analogy, loving parents sometimes allow their children to suffer evil or pain out of respect for their freedom and so that their children can mature in certain ways. This does not show that parents do not love their children or that they do not have the power to intervene; rather, it emphasizes their love for their children, including a love for their freedom.

In the Christian understanding, moreover, suffering and death do not have the final say. Christ's Resurrection demonstrates that death and evil ultimately fail; Christ takes upon himself the consequences of our sin, our death, and our suffering, and transforms them, hallows them, and fills them with meaning. See *How can a good and all-powerful God allow suffering?* (page 47) for a discussion of this question.

Reply to Objection 5: The claims about Jesus are childish fantasy.
There are many rational reasons for believing in the Resurrection of Christ. The Apostles and other witnesses—and the absence of contrary evidence at the time of the Resurrection—provide credible testimony that Christ truly rose from the dead. People do not mistake a dead man for a living one. The Christian faith is not an abstraction but is based in historical fact. See *Was the Resurrection a literal, historical event?* (page 17) for more information about this question.

Moreover, our experience of sin and our need for God to forgive us provide a basis for the intelligibility of the Incarnation and the claims of the Christian faith. These claims are backed up by historical data as well as the evidence of miracles, especially well-documented Eucharistic miracles and miracles of healing that emerge in the canonization process. The claims of faith are above all verified by the testimony and lives of Christian saints, both at the time of Christ and since.

FURTHER STUDY

Catechism of the Catholic Church, §§27–43.

Catholic Answers at Catholic.com

- James Kidd, "A Proof of the Existence of God," May 1, 2006.

- Cale Clarke, "C. S. Lewis and the Argument from Morality to God," August 16, 2017.

- Trent Horn, "Arguments For (and Against) the Existence of God," December 1, 2017.

- Douglas M. Beaumont, "Clarifying Arguments for God" (Three Parts), June 18, 2019.

- Edward Feser, "Proofs for the Existence of God," September 8, 2017.

Scott Hahn and Benjamin Wiker, *Answering the New Atheism: Dismantling Dawkins' Case Against God* (Steubenville, Ohio: Emmaus Road Publishing, 2008).

Peter Kreeft, "The Reasons to Believe," in *Catholic Controversies: Understanding Church Teachings and Events in History*, ed. Stephen Gabriel (Falls Church, Virginia: Moorings Press, 2010), 18–34.

Peter Kreeft and Ronald K. Tacelli, S.J., "Twenty Arguments for the Existence of God," in *Handbook of Christian Apologetics: Hundreds of Answers to Crucial Questions* (Downers Grove, Illinois: InterVarsity Press, 1994), 47–88.

RESURRECTION

Was the Resurrection a literal, historical event?

Objection 1
Rising from the dead is contrary to the laws of nature. Witnesses of Jesus' "Resurrection" must therefore have witnessed something other than a literal return to life. Any possible alternatives are more plausible than an impossible claim.

Objection 2
The Gospels are unreliable as historical texts since they are filled with inconsistencies and factual and scientific errors. Many of these inconsistencies are likely due to the length of time between actual events and their written accounts. Since the authors of the Gospels lacked direct exposure to the Apostles and were dependent on later oral narratives, their descriptions of the Resurrection cannot be relied upon as accurate.

Objection 3
The Gospels were never intended to be taken literally. They convey spiritual, not historical, realities. Myth-making was a common practice in the ancient world, especially to reveal religious truths. The Resurrection of Jesus was one of those myths.

Objection 4
The Gospel accounts are deceptive. They were deliberately fabricated to sustain the credibility of Jesus and his followers after the Crucifixion. In his teaching, Jesus had styled himself as the Jewish Messiah, a Davidic king who would restore God's kingdom on earth. Like so many other messianic figures of his day, Jesus failed, prompting his disciples to construct a narrative that would validate continued belief in his mission. Part of that narrative was the Resurrection.

Objection 5
Some claim that the willingness of Jesus' disciples to be martyred

demonstrates that they truly believed in the Resurrection. However, even in modern times large groups of people have been willing to die for the sake of delusions, such as the 909 suicides from poisoned Kool-Aid in 1978 in Jonestown, Guyana. Neither is the rapid rise of Christian faith in the face of persecution evidence of a literal Resurrection; other faiths, such as Islam and Buddhism, rose rapidly in similar circumstances.

CATHOLIC TEACHING

+ Christians believe that the Scriptures accurately record the literal Resurrection of Jesus. "The Resurrection of Jesus is the crowning truth of our faith in Christ, a faith believed and lived as the central truth by the first Christian community" (CCC §638). We believe in the Resurrection above all through faith, through the Word of God which never deceives.

+ However, **even without a belief in the reliability of Scripture, a literal Resurrection is the most plausible explanation for the account recorded by historical documents.**

+ For example, the Gospels represent **multiple historical documents** claiming that the Resurrection occurred. Even presuming inconsistencies within the accounts, they are remarkably harmonious on the key facts, such as the empty tomb, the Resurrection, and the post-Resurrection appearances.

+ The Gospels are of a genre that **valued historical accuracy.** Indeed, other writings of this time period, such as those of Jewish historian Josephus and Greek historians Herodotus and Thucydides, are used by modern historians as valid sources of historical data.

+ It would have been **easy to contest** the clear and bold claims of the Gospels, especially by non-believing Jewish and Roman authorities. If the Resurrection were not a literal event, the body of Jesus would have refuted the claim of the empty tomb. **If the claim that five hundred people saw Jesus after his death were untrue, it would have been simple to challenge it.** There is no evidence of such challenges being made.

+ Other evidence corroborates the validity of the Christian claim. For instance, there were many other **messianic figures** at the time of Jesus, and yet the world knows only of Jesus. Also, **many Christian martyrs** went to their deaths willingly, even joyfully, for holding to the literal Resurrection. Finally, **Christianity expanded quickly even in the midst of severe persecution**. None of these are definitive, but taken together they bolster the credibility of early Christian belief in Jesus' Resurrection.

+ From a psychological point of view, it is **highly unlikely that the Resurrection was fabricated or the product of mass delusion**. It is too central an element of the Christian message to attribute to cunning teams of conspirators or to group self-deception. There are simply too many ways that such a hoax would eventually have been exposed, and mass delusions do not last for centuries.

REPLY

Reply to Objection 1: Resurrection is impossible because it is contrary to laws of nature.
This objection fails by its circular reasoning. It is equivalent to saying, "This miracle didn't happen because miracles don't happen." Evidence to the contrary is willfully ignored.

Reply to Objection 2: The Gospel accounts are inconsistent and unreliable.
Scholars have shown that apparent inconsistencies in the Gospels can, in fact, be reconciled. Apart from that question, however, minor inconsistencies in the Resurrection accounts do not disprove the much deeper harmony of the texts. In fact, they reinforce it. Witnesses in court are not deemed unreliable because their accounts have slight inconsistencies. Trivial disparities among witnesses makes their testimony more credible, not less, since it shows they did not coordinate their responses. The fact that the Gospels have minor inconsistencies simply means that they are drawing from various eye-witnesses, adding to their historical reliability. The fact that the Church did not modify those obvious inconsistencies while insisting upon the basic historical claims further reinforces the reliability of the accounts. Lastly, while it is true that the Gospels were written down some decades after the events took place, they were written in the lifetimes of eye-witnesses. Seeing a man return to life is not a detail that one forgets or confuses with the passage of time. It either happened or it didn't, and the

Gospel accounts are unanimous and emphatic in reporting that it did.

Reply to Objection 3: The Gospels are not intended to be taken literally.
People in the ancient world were as capable as people in the modern world of distinguishing fact from fiction. That the Apostles were willing to be martyred and allow their followers to be martyred demonstrates that they were convinced of the historical truth of the Gospels, including the Resurrection. People do not shed their blood by the thousands defending the historical claims of a fictional story.

Reply to Objection 4: The Resurrection was an intentional deception by the disciples of Jesus.
The claim of conspiracy is a logical but not very credible possibility. First of all, if early Christians were seeking to promulgate a lie, they would have had no problem doctoring texts for consistency, as noted above. The fact that they did not suggests that such a conspiracy did not exist. In addition, the charge of conspiracy is so implausible that its very consideration betrays ideological partiality. To summarize: a small band of unlearned men, mainly fishermen, invented the greatest lie of all time, proclaimed in the very generation as the event itself, in the face of hostile local and imperial authorities who could have debunked it in countless different ways but chose not to, in a conspiracy so airtight that we have not a shred of evidence for it, without a single conspirator betraying the others or the ruse itself, and virtually every one of them was tortured and killed for refusing to break confidence. This elaborate hoax has changed world history for two thousand years. Is this vast conspiracy without proof a more plausible account than the simple explanation that the Resurrection might actually be true?

Reply to Objection 5: The later behavior of the Apostles is not reliable evidence for the Resurrection.
It is true that the willingness of the Apostles to be martyred does not itself demonstrate the truth of the Resurrection. The argument for the literal truth of the Resurrection relies not on a single point of data but on credible documentary evidence and a calm and rational evaluation of those documents and the historical record. It is a larger historical picture, based on solid evidence, that reinforces the bold claim of the early Christian community. The contrary case, that the Resurrection was not an historical event, would need minimal, though credible, evidence to discredit the Resurrection accounts. None has emerged.

FURTHER STUDY

Catechism of the Catholic Church, §§638–647.

Catholic Answers at Catholic.com

+ Trent Horn, "Christ's Resurrection: Bodily or Only Spiritual?" April 14, 2020.

+ Karlo Broussard, "Why the Resurrection Was Not a Conspiracy," March 30, 2016.

+ Karlo Broussard, "Biblical Resurrection Reports Are Not 'Hopelessly Contradictory,'" July 11, 2017.

+ Karlo Broussard, "Is the Resurrection a Lie?" November 19, 2018.

Richard Bauckham, *Jesus and the Eyewitnesses: The Gospels as Eyewitness Testimony* (Grand Rapids, Michigan: Eerdmans, 2017).

Peter Kreeft and Ronald K. Tacelli, S.J., "The Resurrection," in *Handbook of Christian Apologetics: Hundreds of Answers to Crucial Questions* (Downers Grove, Illinois: InterVarsity Press, 1994), 175–198.

PRAYING TO
THE SAINTS

Why do Catholics pray to the saints?

Objection 1
Praying to the saints diminishes the honor that we owe to God.

Objection 2
Christ is the sole mediator of redemption. "For there is one God, and there is one mediator between God and men, the man Christ Jesus" (1 Tim 2:5; see also Heb 9:15 and 12:24). Praying to the saints implies that there are additional mediators.

Objection 3
Even if we could pray to saints, there would be no point to it, since we are asking them to pray to God for us. We can simply pray to God ourselves.

Objection 4
God has forbidden necromancy, or contact with the dead (see Deut 18:10–12). Praying to the saints—that is, those who have died—is a form of necromancy.

Objection 5
Saints cannot hear us in heaven and could not understand or answer so many prayers if they did. Thus it is unreasonable to pray to saints.

Objection 6
Images of the saints (which foster intercessory prayer) are against the Second Commandment forbidding "graven images" (Exod 20:4).

Objection 7
Praying to saints was a later innovation and not practiced in the early Church.

CATHOLIC TEACHING

+ **Jesus is the sole mediator of redemption for the human race. Nevertheless, Jesus himself asks us to pray for each other** (see Matt 5:44). He frequently answered prayers based on another person's faith (see Matt 8:13, 15:28, 17:15). Praying for others, then, cannot undermine Christ's sole mediatorship.

+ From the Church's earliest days, **Christians have prayed for others** (see Acts 12:5; 2 Cor 9:14; 2 Thess 1:11, etc.). It is an act of faith as well as charity—and even justice—that we do so.

+ As evidenced by votive offerings to the saints from ancient times, **the Church has always believed that this power to intercede does not end at death.** Early Christians were known, for instance, to slip prayer intentions to martyrs on their way to execution, hoping that they would offer those prayers to God once they were in his presence.

+ The saints, like us, are members of the Church and pray for their brothers and sisters on earth. In the words of the Letter to the Hebrews, "We are surrounded by so great a cloud of witnesses" who inspire us to "run with perseverance the race that is set before us" (Heb 12:1).

+ Asking for the intercession of the saints is an act of piety. Piety refers not only to honoring God as Father but also to honoring people who somehow share in his care and love. The Fourth Commandment, for instance, specifies that children should honor their parents. Citizens should honor public officials. Parishioners should honor their pastors. **Saints, too, should be honored by Christians** on earth, who acknowledge the saints' closeness to God and their desire and ability to intercede for us. Such veneration of the saints is distinct from the adoration that is owed to God alone.

REPLY

Reply to Objection 1: Honoring the saints diminishes the honor that we owe to God.

Praying to the saints does not lessen our reverence for God. On the contrary, by acknowledging the power of God's grace that redeemed and sanctified the saints, we honor God by venerating his saints as we honor parents when we respect their children. In addition, when God uses human instruments (including those in heaven) to carry out his will, his greatness is amplified, not diminished. To use an analogy, a great king might accomplish his will through many ambassadors and officials. His majesty and power are magnified, not undermined, by his use of these "secondary causes" of his kingship.

Reply to Objection 2: Christ is the sole mediator.

Praying to the saints cannot oppose Christ's unique mediatorship since he himself commands us to pray for one another. Such a command does not cease with death. Saints are collaborators, not rivals, with Jesus in the work of redemption.

Reply to Objection 3: We should pray to God alone.

God would not ask us to pray for one another if there were no point in it. Jesus desires us to be participants in the work of redemption, as he instructed and prepared his disciples to carry on his mission. "Go therefore and make disciples of all nations" (Matt 28:19), he told them. He invites them into his mission, demonstrating that he wishes them to be cooperators in his work of redemption. Similarly, he wishes us to pray for one another as participants in his salvific work. None would fulfill that command so perfectly as those who are already perfected and dwelling in his presence.

Reply to Objection 4: Praying to the saints is a form of necromancy.

God has forbidden the practice of calling up spirits from the dead. Since the saints are living in glory, asking for their prayers does not summon them from the dead. In addition, necromancy is an act that seeks to exploit the spiritual world for personal gain. Even when those motives are well-intentioned, the exercise of necromancy is an act of domination and control over spirits. In contrast, asking for the intercession of the saints, who are always in union with God's will, is an act of humility and faith.

Reply to Objection 5: Saints could never hear or answer so many prayers.

Such an objection reveals a limited view of life in heaven. Saints are not subject to the same limitations of time and place that we are on earth, who can generally do only one thing at a time. In the Beatific Vision, saints see and hear all that God desires them to see and hear, including the many prayers expressed in faith by men and women on earth.

Reply to Objection 6: God forbids graven images.
The Second Commandment does not forbid all images but only those which could obscure the transcendence of God or which could be worshipped in place of God. The Catechism observes that "already in the Old Testament, God ordained or permitted the making of images that pointed symbolically toward salvation by the incarnate Word: so it was with the bronze serpent, the ark of the covenant, and the cherubim" (CCC §2130, see Num 21:8–9; Exod 25:10–22; 1 Kgs 6:23–28). Images of the saints are not adored as God; they are honored as representing the masterpieces of his grace. Holy images help us honor and follow our ancestors in the family of faith.

Reply to Objection 7: Praying to the saints is a later innovation of the Church.
Clear evidence of votive offerings to the saints (for instance, at the ancient tomb of St. Peter) shows that Christians from the earliest days understood that their prayers could be heard by saintly souls in heaven. There is abundant proof of this practice from ancient writings that reflect an unwavering and confident hope in the intercessory power of saints. St. Cyprian of Carthage, to take one example, writes in the mid-200s that "if any one of us, blessed through God's favor with a speedy death, should go on ahead before the others, let our charity continue still before the presence of the Lord, let our prayers not cease on behalf of our brothers and sisters in the presence of our merciful Father."[1] St. Augustine encourages the memorials of the martyrs so that the Christian people can "pay religious honor to the memory of the martyrs, both to excite us to imitate them, and to obtain a share in their merits, and the assistance of their prayers."[2] Praying to the saints is not a later innovation of the Church but a practice that the earliest Christians saw as the natural complement to their faith in the afterlife.

---

[1] St. Cyprian of Carthage, *The Letters of St. Cyprian of Carthage*, trans. G.W. Clarke, vol. 3 (New York: Newman Press, 1986), 92.

[2] St. Augustine, *Nicene and Post-Nicene Fathers*, ed. Philip Schaff, vol. 4 (Peabody, MA: Hendrickson Publishers, 2004), 262. Reprint of the same volume published by the Christian Literature Publishing Company in 1887.

FURTHER STUDY

Catechism of the Catholic Church, §§946–959.

Catholic Answers at Catholic.com

- ✦ "Why Do Catholics Pray to Saints?" Tract, August 10, 2004.

- ✦ Karlo Broussard, "Catholics Pray to Jesus and to the Saints," August 10, 2020.

- ✦ Karlo Broussard, "The Saints Hear Our Prayers and Intercede for Us," May 20, 2019.

- ✦ "What the Early Church Believed: The Intercession of the Saints," Tract, August 10, 2004.

Scott Hahn, *Angels and Saints: A Biblical Guide to Friendship with God's Holy Ones* (New York: Image, 2014).

Staff of Catholic Answers, "Praying to the Saints," in *The Essential Catholic Survival Guide: Answers to Tough Questions About the Faith* (San Diego: Catholic Answers, 2005), 91–97.

Patrick Madrid, "The Saints," in *Where is That in the Bible?* (Huntington, Indiana: Our Sunday Visitor Publishing Division, 2001), 58–61.

MARIAN DEVOTION

Why do Catholics have a special veneration for Mary?

Objection 1
The Catholic Church fosters an exaggerated regard for Mary. Calling her the "Mother of God," for instance, is manifestly erroneous. God has no mother; God is the uncreated Creator. The title is, therefore, either ignorant or blasphemous.

Objection 2
The "Immaculate Conception" alleges that Mary was conceived without sin and committed no personal sin. Yet St. Paul says that "all have sinned and fall short of the glory of God" (Rom 3:23) and St. John adds that "if we say we have no sin, we deceive ourselves" (1 John 1:8). Thus Mary, too, sinned and needed to be redeemed.

Objection 3
The "Perpetual Virginity" denies that Mary had other children. However, Jesus' own contemporaries refuted this claim when they asked, are "not his brethren James and Joseph and Simon and Judas? And are not all his sisters with us?" (Matt 13:55–56). In addition, when Joseph took Mary as his wife, the Scriptures state that he "knew her not *until* she had borne a son" (Matt 1:25), clearly suggesting that they had marital relations after she bore Jesus.

Objection 4
The "Assumption" claims that Mary was taken body and soul to heaven at the end of her life. Yet St. John teaches that "no one has ascended into heaven but he who descended from heaven, the Son of man" (John 3:13), and St. Paul writes that all will rise in Christ but "each in his own order: Christ the first fruits, then *at his coming* those who belong to Christ" (1 Cor 15:23). Thus Mary could not have "risen in Christ"—or been assumed into heaven—before Christ's return.

Objection 5
These and other teachings on Mary are found nowhere in the Bible. They are therefore not part of the Christian faith.

CATHOLIC TEACHING

+ **The first expression of Marian devotion was from the Archangel Gabriel**: "Hail, full of grace, the Lord is with you!" (Luke 1:28). Nowhere in the Bible is anyone addressed by an angel in such deferential terms. The very phrase "full of grace," used nowhere else in Scripture, has the construction of a personal name for Mary used by the Archangel. The second instance of Marian devotion is from St. Elizabeth who, "filled with the Holy Spirit," cried out, "Blessed are you among women" (Luke 1:41–42). Mary herself humbly acknowledges that "henceforth all generations will call me blessed" (Luke 1:48).

+ **From the earliest days of the Church, Christians have instinctively venerated Mary**, the mother of Jesus. Each of her titles emerged as the fruit of prayer, from the life of worship, and through the guidance of the Church's authoritative teaching. **Christians honor Mary in imitation of their Lord**, who loved his mother on earth and, in perfect obedience to the Fourth Commandment, continues to honor her in heaven.

REPLY

Reply to Objection 1: God has no mother.
Identifying Mary as "Mother of God" is not, as it would be in humans, claiming that she is the generator of God, who of course has no origin. It is rather an affirmation that she is the mother of Jesus and simultaneously that his two natures, divine and human, are united in one person. If Mary is not also the Mother of God, then quite simply, Jesus is not God. This title is suggested in the Scriptures when St. Elizabeth calls the Blessed Virgin "the mother of my Lord" (Luke 1:43).

Reply to Objection 2: Everyone, including Mary, is a sinner and needs to be redeemed.
The teaching of St. Paul that "all have sinned" and of St. John that "we deceive ourselves" if anyone claims to be sinless, clearly cannot refer

only to personal sin. After all, infants have not personally sinned. Rather, these statements affirm that everyone must be redeemed from sin itself, from original sin, and Mary is no exception. The Immaculate Conception does not deny that Mary, like all human beings, needed a redeemer and savior. Mary was redeemed by the grace of Christ, but in an anticipatory way so that she would be a fit dwelling for the Incarnate Lord as the Ark of the New Covenant (see reply to objection 4, below). This is the reason for St. Gabriel's remarkable salutation of Mary as "full of grace." As John the Baptist was sanctified in the womb prior to his birth (see Luke 1:15), so Mary was sanctified at her very conception.

Reply to Objection 3: Scripture shows that Mary had other children besides Jesus.
Without the consistent testimony of the ancient Church about the perpetual virginity of Mary, the "brothers and sisters" of the Lord could indeed refer to other children of hers. However, it should be noted that the Hebrew language had no words for cousins, nephews, or uncles, so the term "brothers" in the Scriptures often refers not to blood-brothers but rather cousins, half-siblings, or other relatives (see, for instance, Gen 29:15 in which Abraham calls his nephew Lot his "brother").

In addition, the statement that St. Joseph "knew [Mary] not *until* she had borne a son" is ambiguous. It is above all a reference to the title of "firstborn son" (see Exod 22:29), which foreshadows the redemptive work of Christ. In the Old Testament context, having a "firstborn" does not imply that there will be other children. Secondly, the Scriptures furnish many uses of the word "until" that do not suggest future behavior. For instance, St. Paul writes, "*Till* I come, attend to the public reading of Scripture, to preaching, to teaching" (1 Tim 4:13), which does not mean that Timothy should cease preaching after Paul arrives!

Finally, that Jesus had no blood brothers and sisters is implicit in his decision to entrust Mary to John at the foot of the Cross (John 19:26). Other children of Mary, if there were any, would certainly have taken care of her after Jesus' death. The teaching on Mary's perpetual virginity is so well-founded that even the principal Protestant leaders (Luther, Calvin, Zwingli) held to the teaching and declared it the teaching of the Bible.

Reply to Objection 4: No one can ascend into heaven until Christ's return.
It is important to note that Mary, unlike Jesus, did not *ascend* on her
own power, but rather she was *assumed* into heaven by God. St. Paul's
statement in 1 Corinthians 15:23 refers to the general resurrection,
which Mary experienced in anticipation, as indeed Enoch and Elijah
did in the Old Testament (see Gen 5:24; 2 Kgs 2:11).

The Assumption of Mary complements her Immaculate Conception.
Bodily corruption seems unfitting for the woman fashioned so care-
fully by God to be the sinless mother of his Son. More importantly,
the Assumption is strongly suggested by the New Testament identification of Mary as the Ark of the New Covenant. In the Old Covenant, the ark held three items (see Heb 9:4): manna (the bread from
heaven), the Ten Commandments (the Word of God), and the rod of
Aaron (representing the Aaronic priesthood). Mary, as the New Ark,
carried in her womb the fulfillment of all three: Jesus who is the "true
bread from heaven" (John 6:32), the "Word become flesh" (John 1:14),
and the "high priest of our confession" (Heb 3:1). The Gospel makes
clear that when she visits her cousin Elizabeth, Mary is the living Ark
of the New Covenant. Elizabeth's words echo almost precisely those
of King David, "How can the ark of the Lord come to me?" (2 Sam
6:9; compare to Luke 1:43) and, like the ark of old, Mary stayed with
Elizabeth for three months (2 Sam 6:11; compare to Luke 1:56). She
is therefore the New Ark, and as Revelation makes clear, the Ark is in
"God's temple in heaven" (Rev 11:19).

A final argument for the Assumption can be found in history. The
bones and relics of saints from every region and walk of life were
ardently revered by Christians from a very early date. Surely those
of the Lord's own mother would have been the most prized treasures
of Christians anywhere. There is no hint, however, of Mary's relics
being venerated by any Christians at any time. They were not venerated because they were not on earth.

Reply to Objection 5: Catholic teachings on Mary are unscriptural.
See *Is Scripture the only rule of faith?* (page 97) for a response to this
and similar objections.

FURTHER STUDY

Catechism of the Catholic Church, §§963–972.

Catholic Answers at Catholic.com

- "What the Early Church Believed: Mary is the Mother of God," Tract, August 10, 2004.

- Jason Evert, "How to Explain the Perpetual Virginity of Mary," July 1, 2000.

- Tim Staples, "Mary, Mother of God," October 12, 2013.

- Jason Evert, "How to Argue for Mary's Assumption," May 1, 2001.

- Fr. Dwight Longenecker, "How to Explain Mary to a Sola Scriptura Protestant," January 1, 2003.

Scott Hahn, *Hail, Holy Queen: The Mother of God in the Word of God* (New York: Image, 2006).

John Hampsch, *Scriptural Basis for Marian Doctrine and Devotion: Questions and Answers* (Goleta, California: Queenship Publishing, 1995).

Staff of Catholic Answers, "Brethren of the Lord," in *The Essential Catholic Survival Guide: Answers to Tough Questions About the Faith* (San Diego: Catholic Answers, 2005), 119–125.

Staff of Catholic Answers, "Immaculate Conception and Assumption," in *The Essential Catholic Survival Guide: Answers to Tough Questions About the Faith* (San Diego: Catholic Answers, 2005), 126–132.

Mark Shea, "The Mother of the Son: The Case for Marian Devotion," in *Catholic Controversies: Understanding Church Teachings and Events in History*, ed. Stephen Gabriel (Falls Church, Virginia: Moorings Press, 2010), 324–334.

Patrick Madrid, "The Blessed Virgin Mary," in *Answer Me This!* (Huntington, Indiana: Our Sunday Visitor Publishing Division, 2003), 134–167.

PURGATORY

Why do Catholics believe in purgatory?

Objection 1
The Bible does not mention purgatory. Since all that is essential to our salvation is contained in the Holy Scriptures, purgatory either does not exist or is not relevant to our salvation.

Objection 2
The primary text cited by Catholics in their defense of purgatory is from 2 Maccabees, which is not canonical and hence non-scriptural.

Objection 3
The notion of purgatory relies on an erroneous view of justification. By asserting that souls must suffer in purgatory for sins, the doctrine implies that the work of Christ is not finished and that we must complete his sacrificial work through works and suffering. This is tantamount to saying that the redemption of Jesus was not sufficient and that we must earn heaven on our own. Thus purgatory is not only unnecessary; it also contradicts God's Word. As the Bible teaches, "Where there is forgiveness . . . there is no longer any offering for sin" (Heb 10:18).

Objection 4
The Church invented purgatory in the sixteenth century to raise money by selling indulgences.

CATHOLIC TEACHING

- **The Scriptures teach that not all sin is deadly.** St. John teaches this explicitly in 1 John 5:16–17 and St. James writes that "sin fully grown brings forth death" (Jas 1:15), clearly implying that there is sin which is *not* fully grown and has *not* brought forth death. **Purgatory is the way God has chosen to purify us of non-deadly (venial) sins and the residual effects of forgiven sin**, what is called the "temporal punishment due to sin." **It is not a "second chance" for those who die in a state of mortal sin.**

- Juxtaposed to this teaching on non-deadly sin is the **extremely high standard by which Jesus measures our suitability for heaven.** He tells his disciples, "You, therefore, must be perfect, as your heavenly Father is perfect" (Matt 5:48). The Book of Revelation affirms that "nothing unclean shall enter" the heavenly Jerusalem (Rev 21:27). In fact, many have speculated that the holiness of heaven would torture or even annihilate a soul less than perfect. St. John Henry Newman declared that "Heaven would be hell to an irreligious man."[1]

- Purgatory is the doctrine which bridges these truths about human sinfulness and the sinlessness demanded of the saints. **It is the merciful plan of Providence to purify imperfect souls of their attachments to venial sins as well as the temporal effects of their forgiven sins, making them fit for heaven.** It is a state or place of purification for souls who have died in a state of grace and hence are assured of their salvation but are not yet ready for heaven.

REPLY

Reply to Objection 1: Purgatory is not mentioned in the Scriptures.
It is true that the word "purgatory" does not occur in the Bible. Nor do the words "Trinity" or "Incarnation" or even "Bible." Nevertheless, there is abundant evidence in Scripture for the doctrine. To begin, the notion that there can be a temporary state after death which is neither heaven nor hell is suggested in several Gospel passages (e.g.

---

[1] St. John Henry Newman, "Holiness Necessary for Future Blessedness," in *Plain and Parochial Sermons*, vol. 1 (London: Longmans, Green, and Co., 1907), 7.

Matt 5:21–26; Matt 18:34; Luke 12:58–59; Luke 16:19–31), and St. Peter affirms that Christ preached the Gospel to "the dead" and the "disobedient spirits" (see 1 Pet 3:18–20; 1 Pet 4:6). There are other examples. Jesus warns that those who sin against the Holy Spirit will not be forgiven, "either in this age or in the age to come" (Matt 12:32). St. Paul warns that the man who builds his work on a spiritually weak foundation "will suffer loss, though he himself will be saved, but only as through fire" (1 Cor 3:15). The most explicit reference to purgatory, however, is 2 Maccabees 12:42–45, in which Judas Maccabaeus explicitly prays for the souls of his soldiers who died sinfully but who nonetheless "fell asleep in godliness," and he sends a collection to Jerusalem so that a "sin offering" might be made on their behalf. The sacred writer states that "if he were not expecting that those who had fallen would rise again, it would have been superfluous and foolish to pray for the dead. . . . Therefore he made atonement for the dead, that they might be delivered from their sin."

Reply to Objection 2: The Maccabean text cited in defense of purgatory is not in the canonical Scriptures.
It was not until the Reformation that large numbers of Christians denied certain books of the Old Testament, ostensibly for historical reasons, but also because the Scriptures did not accord with Protestant doctrines. Arguably it is this text from Maccabees more than any other that collided with Luther's theory of "justification by faith alone." The Book of Maccabees, however, is in the Greek Septuagint, the version of the Old Testament used by the Church from the beginning, indeed by Christ himself (e.g. Luke 4:16–19; Mark 7:6–7) and by all the New Testament writers. Hebrews 11:35 cites the book of Maccabees itself. Indeed, there were scores of books in the ancient world purporting to be valid Christian Scriptures, and it was only the authority of the Church that was able to confirm the true canon of inspired texts. When Protestants use the Bible to attack these "apocryphal" books or Catholic doctrines such as purgatory, they are using the very Bible that Catholic bishops ratified.

Reply to Objection 3: Purgatory suggests that Christ's redemptive work is incomplete.
The Catholic Church teaches that Christ certainly did pay the dreadful price for all our sins. Nevertheless, we cooperate in our own redemption through the process of sanctification. In the words of St. Augustine, "God created us without us: but he did not will to save

us without us."[2] The grace that Christ obtained on the Cross is not merely applied to us as "snow covering manure," in an expression often attributed to Martin Luther. Sanctifying grace actually changes us to the core of our being; the process of sanctification is the working out in our lives of the grace that Christ won for us on the Cross. Hence purgatory, which completes the work of sanctification in our souls by removing the vestiges of self-love, does not deny the sufficiency of Christ's redemption but rather emphasizes it. In addition, there is "temporal punishment" of sin that is not eliminated by God's pardon. Sin is not primarily a legal infraction but a lingering wound in our relationship with God, and we have to heal those wounds in this life through our prayers, sacrifices, and works of charity. To use an analogy from human justice, a boy can be forgiven for hitting a baseball through a window, but he still has to pay for a new window! When we don't pay for the "broken window" in this life, God, in his great mercy, gives us a chance to do so in the next. That is purgatory.

Reply to Objection 4: The teaching on purgatory is a later innovation of the Church.
It cannot be said that purgatory is a later invention of the Church. To begin, even if one were to reject the canonicity of Maccabees, that sacred book no doubt reflects the religious beliefs of the Jews a little over a hundred years *before* Christ: that they prayed for the dead—as many still do today. The idea was prevalent at the time of Jesus already. Moreover, ancient Christian liturgies and tomb inscriptions from the second and third centuries include prayers for the dead. Tertullian in AD 211 mentions praying and sacrificing for the dead as an established custom, demonstrating that the teaching was universal in the Church fourteen centuries before the Reformation. In the fourth century, St. Monica asked her son St. Augustine to remember her soul in his Masses after she died. In addition, Christians in the early centuries were strident and even violent in defending the traditional faith handed on to them. If purgatory were a doctrinal innovation or if Rome invented it to establish a system of paid indulgences to raise money, there would certainly have been protests, but there is no evidence, at any time, that any early Christians objected to the universal belief in praying for the dead or that the dead could be aided by our prayers, which is incontrovertible evidence that they believed in the doctrine of purgatory.

---

[2]   St. Augustine, *Sermon* 169, 11, 13: PL 38, 923 (cited in CCC §1847).

FURTHER STUDY

Catechism of the Catholic Church, §§1030–1032.

Catholic Answers at Catholic.com

- "What Does the Catholic Church Teach About Purgatory?" Tract, August 10, 2004.

- Tim Staples, "Is Purgatory in the Bible?" January 17, 2014.

- "What the Early Church Believed: Purgatory," Tract, August 10, 2004.

- Karlo Broussard, "Does Purgatory Deny Christ's Sacrifice?" October 29, 2018.

Staff of Catholic Answers, "Purgatory," in *The Essential Catholic Survival Guide: Answers to Tough Questions About the Faith* (San Diego: Catholic Answers, 2005), 250–256.

Mark P. Shea, "Purgatory? Where is *That* in the Bible?" in *Catholic Controversies: Understanding Church Teachings and Events in History*, ed. Stephen Gabriel (Falls Church, Virginia: Moorings Press, 2010), 367–376.

Patrick Madrid, "Purgatory," in *Does the Bible Really Say That?: Discovering Catholic Teaching in Scripture* (Cincinnati: Servant, 2006), 95–98.

Patrick Madrid, "Purgatory," in *Answer Me This!* (Huntington, Indiana: Our Sunday Visitor Publishing Division, 2003), 199–208.

HELL

Can we really believe in eternal punishment for sinners?

Objection 1
The Scriptures make clear that God "desires all men to be saved and to come to the knowledge of the truth" (1 Tim 2:4; see also 2 Pet 3:9). Since God wills it and he is omnipotent, it follows that all are saved, and hence either hell does not exist or it is not eternal.

Objection 2
Subjecting sinners to eternal punishment without reprieve and without end is the act of a merciless tyrant. The Church teaches that one mortal sin at the end of one's life, even after a long life of virtuous deeds, merits hell. Such exacting punishment is unreasonable and contrary to Jesus' revelation of a merciful Father.

Objection 3
Original sin has compromised our ability to comprehend the gravity of sin and resist its allure. Since we are guilty of mortal sin only when we have full knowledge and consent of the will, it is likely that mortal sin rarely, if ever, occurs. Even if it did, it would only be through the weakness of original sin—for which we are not culpable. Thus it would be unjust to punish sinners with eternal damnation. Since God is not unjust, an eternal hell cannot exist.

Objection 4
The Bible teaches that God will "wipe away every tear" from the eyes of the saints and "neither shall there be mourning nor crying" (Rev 21:4). However, the eternal agony of the damned would surely be a source of sorrow for the saints. Thus the blessedness of the saints is itself proof against an eternal hell.

Objection 5
Jesus "descended into the lower parts of the earth" (Eph 4:9) and "preached [the Gospel] even to the dead" (1 Pet 4:6). This "harrow-

ing of hell" commemorated on Holy Saturday refutes the notion that souls in hell cannot repent and be saved.

CATHOLIC TEACHING

+ **All, even those who do not know Christ, are given the help necessary to attain salvation.**[1] No one is outside the embrace of God's love and his desire for their salvation.

+ Nevertheless, **salvation is never forced upon us.** We are invited to freely accept or reject God and are not obliged to choose salvation. **The eternity of hell therefore rests upon the dignity of human beings as free, rational, and immortal beings.**

+ Love demands a permanent commitment, a personal choice. This implies the possibility of sin. "Mortal sin is a radical possibility of human freedom, as is love itself. . . . our freedom has the power to make choices forever, with no turning back" (CCC §1861). **To sin is to choose against a loving commitment to God.** "To die in mortal sin without repenting and accepting God's merciful love," the Catechism teaches, "means remaining separated from him forever by our own free choice. This state of definitive self-exclusion from communion with God and the blessed is called 'hell'" (CCC §1033; also see 1 John 5:16).

+ **Sin is an offense not only against love but also against justice.** It is a rejection of God's holiness. Since there is a proportion between the gravity of an offense and its punishment, a definitive offense against the infinite holiness and majesty of God can only be punished in an equally definitive way, which is hell.

+ The teaching on hell is **a call to personal responsibility and conversion.** It calls man to make good "use of his freedom in view of his eternal destiny" (CCC §1036).

+ **The reality of hell is taught throughout Scripture and especially by Jesus himself, who called it "the eternal fire" (Matt 25:41).** See also, for instance, Matthew 5:22, 29, 10:28, 13:41–

---

[1] See Second Vatican Council, Dogmatic Constitution on the Church *Lumen Gentium*, November 21, 1964, §16.

42, 50; Revelation 14:10–11, 20:10. It has been the constant teaching of the Church, despite repeated attempts through the centuries to undermine it, that "each man receives punishment or salvation according to the merits of his actions," as St. Justin Martyr wrote in the second century.[2] It has also been part of the messages of Marian apparitions through the centuries, notably Our Lady of Fatima, who asked St. Jacinta to "pray very much, because so many souls are going to hell because so few people are praying and offering sacrifice for them."

REPLY

Reply to Objection 1: God wills all to be saved.
God wills the salvation of all, but he doesn't force his love upon us. In his goodness he created us as free beings and does not force us to love him in return. Such, indeed, would no longer be love. At death, our decision to love or not love is definitive. At the same time, we do not know who is in hell, which is why the Church prays for all the dead. All are entrusted to the mercy of God who knows the secrets of every heart.

Reply to Objection 2: Hell is incompatible with a merciful God.
The choice for hell lies in the damned, not in God. "It is the *irrevocable* character of their choice," the Catechism teaches about the fall of the angels, "and not a defect in the infinite divine mercy, that makes the angels' sin unforgivable" (CCC §393). The Catechism then quotes St. John Damascene: "There is no repentance for the angels after their fall, just as there is no repentance for men after death."[3] The measure of hell is the measure of the divine love that is offered to all men and women. Hell is the just punishment for the prodigious malice of sin, even as heaven is the indescribable gift to those who choose to love God. However difficult for us to comprehend, the justice of God is never in conflict with his mercy.

Reply to Objection 3: Human beings are not culpable for mortal sin.
Jesus warns us strenuously and frequently about the existence and possibility of hell. He would not do so if it were impossible to go there. Moreover, denying the real human potential for serious sin is tantamount to denying real human freedom and thus human dignity. If we

---

[2] St. Justin Martyr, *The First Apology* (New York: Christian Heritage, 1948), §12.
[3] St. John Damascene, *De Fide orth.* 2, 4: PG 94, 877 (cited in CCC §393).

cannot reject love, neither can we truly choose to love.

Reply to Objection 4: Hell is incompatible with the happiness of the saints.
The saints in heaven perceive the wisdom of God immeasurably better than we do. No one is in hell without fully and completely deserving it. The passions of the saints in heaven, unlike our own, are perfectly aligned with their intellects. They know the full extent of the sinners' rejection of God and perceive, with purity of heart, the justice of their punishment. Hell does not diminish the joy of the saints. It would, after all, be neither just nor merciful for God to permit sinners in hell to "blackmail the universe: that till they consent to be happy (on their own terms) no one else shall taste joy . . . that Hell should be able to veto Heaven."[4]

Reply to Objection 5: Jesus liberated souls in hell on Holy Saturday.
The souls liberated by Jesus after his death were not the souls of the damned but rather those of the just who died before the Incarnation and who awaited their redeemer (see CCC §§631–635). In Scripture this abode of the dead is usually called "Sheol" (Hebrew) and "Hades" (Greek) which is distinguished from "Gehenna," which always refers to the hell of the damned.

---

[4] C. S. Lewis, *The Great Divorce* (New York: Simon & Schuster, 1946), 118.

FURTHER STUDY

Catechism of the Catholic Church, §§1033–1037.

Catholic Answers at Catholic.com

- Tim Staples, "What is Hell?" February 20, 2015.

- Trent Horn, "Yes, Hell is Real and It Is Eternal," September 5, 2019.

- Matt Fradd, "Would God Really Send Someone to Hell?" May 7, 2013.

- Tim Staples, "Are There Souls in Hell Right Now?" April 11, 2014.

- "What the Early Church Believed: Hell," Tract, August 10, 2004.

Peter Kreeft and Ronald K. Tacelli, S.J., "Hell," in *Handbook of Christian Apologetics: Hundreds of Answers to Crucial Questions* (Downers Grove, Illinois: InterVarsity Press, 1994), 280–312.

Patrick Madrid, "Hell," in *Answer Me This!* (Huntington, Indiana: Our Sunday Visitor Publishing Division, 2003), 218–220.

SUFFERING

How can a good and all-powerful God allow suffering?

Objection 1
Any good father, whenever possible, preserves his children from suffering. God, however, does not preserve us from suffering. That means either that he is *unable* to stop our afflictions, or that he is *unwilling* to stop them because he is either evil or indifferent to our pain. Thus suffering is definitive proof that God cannot be both all-powerful and all-good.

Objection 2
God made us for happiness. Suffering, however, is the very opposite of happiness. Thus suffering thwarts God's will, and he would eliminate it if he could.

Objection 3
The Church teaches that suffering is a punishment for original sin. However, we are not responsible for original sin and should not be punished for it. Moreover, some people who suffer—young children for instance—are not responsible even for any personal sin. Thus God punishes innocent people, which shows that he is unjust.

Objection 4
If God is all-powerful, then it must be God's will that people suffer. Now Christians wish to follow the will of God. Alleviating suffering, then, should be forbidden to Christians, which of course is absurd, as the example of Jesus shows. Therefore the premise must be wrong: God cannot will suffering. Its existence must mean that he is unable to stop it.

CATHOLIC TEACHING

+ **Suffering is a profound mystery that challenges all believers.** While reason and revelation can show that suffering is compatible with an all-good, all-powerful God, it cannot "resolve" the mystery of suffering. Ultimately it is a mystery that invites every believer into a deeper level of trust and communion with God. "There is not a single aspect of the Christian message," the Church teaches, "that is not in part an answer to the question of evil" (CCC §309).

+ **Suffering will not last forever.** In the "new heaven and new earth" God "will dwell with" his people and "wipe away every tear from their eyes, and death shall be no more, neither shall there be mourning nor crying nor pain any more" (Rev 21:1, 3, 4).

+ **Some suffering is the consequence of our own free actions**, as when a thief is caught and suffers by going to jail. Even when suffering is the consequence of the free actions of others, it can still be understood as the necessary condition for God to respect the freedom of his human creatures.

+ **The most difficult instance of suffering, however, is the suffering of the innocent**—of young children, for instance. Here we are plunged most deeply into the great mystery of suffering, though always within the context of one overarching principle: that **God would only permit suffering in order to draw forth from it an even greater good.** As St. Paul writes, "in everything God works for good with those who love him" (Rom 8:28). Indeed, this principle is demonstrated most poignantly by the torments and execution of the innocent Jesus. This was the most evil act in history, and from it God drew forth the greatest good, namely the redemption of the human race.

+ We can speculate about some of the "greater goods" that God draws from our suffering. One, for instance, might be faith: suffering can remind us of our need for God. Another might be holiness: suffering helps free us of attachments that keep us from a deeper relationship with God. Yet another might be charity: suffering can increase our capacity to love and draw forth charity from others. **Like human parents with little children, God is able to see farther than we can.** He knows what we truly need for our flourishing in this life and in the next, and sometimes, like a good father, he reluctantly permits suffering so that his children might obtain such goods.

+ **The suffering of Jesus demonstrates that we cannot simply identify suffering as a punishment for personal sin** since Jesus had no sin. Rather his suffering was a sacrifice of love, the consequence of his own fidelity and obedience to the Father's will. His suffering won for us redemption.

+ **By his redemptive suffering, Jesus has shown that Christians can participate in his saving work through their suffering.** St. Paul tells the Colossians, "I rejoice in my sufferings for your sake, and in my flesh I complete what is lacking in Christ's afflictions for the sake of his body, that is, the Church" (Col 1:24; see also 1 Pet 2:21). Christ does not promise to remove our sufferings, then, but rather to transform, to hallow them into a means of sanctification, our own sanctification and that of others.

+ Whatever God's purposes, **suffering is always an invitation to a deeper relationship with Christ.** The witness of the saints through the centuries has shown that suffering, borne for love of God, can be a source of vitality in the Church and even of joy for themselves.

REPLY

Reply to Objection 1: God is unwilling or unable to eliminate suffering. This objection assumes that there is no reason for God to allow suffering, and therefore he cannot be both all-good and all-powerful. However, just as a good father sometimes allows suffering in his children in order to attain a greater good (for instance, when a small child needs a surgical procedure) so, too, does God the Father allow suffering for the sake of greater goods.

Reply to Objection 2: Suffering is the worst evil and thwarts God's will. The worst evil to befall human beings is to be deprived of their ultimate good, which is God himself. However difficult it is to endure suffering, our greatest evil is not suffering: it is sin which separates us from God. The objection is therefore based on a false premise.

Reply to Objection 3: God unjustly punishes innocent people through suffering. Suffering is not a punishment for original sin as if it were a personal fault. Rather, suffering is a consequence of our first parents' choice to separate themselves from God and thereby forfeit his gifts of original holiness and justice. It is their weakened humanity that we have each inherited. Neither is suffering a punishment for personal sin, as the suffering of the sinless Jesus affirms. The suffering of the innocent, then, is not an indictment of God, though it is a deep mystery before which we stand in silence and awe. The Christian teaching never presumes to eliminate or ignore suffering but rather to redeem and sanctify it. It is the suffering of Jesus which gives suffering its meaning and power. Indeed, the fact that many non-believers recoil from suffering and question God's goodness reflects a certain acknowledgement that suffering *ought not to be*, precisely as the Church teaches about fallen nature. There is an implicit acknowledgement of goodness and evil in the very objection, which can become a foundation for faith.

Reply to Objection 4: Since God wills suffering, Christians should too. Suffering is not a good for its own sake but rather only in view of the end for which God permits it. One reason God permits suffering is to draw out the loving care of others. Christians should therefore try—and historically have done, generously and heroically—to diminish the physical, mental, and spiritual suffering of others. The witness of the Church's good works through the centuries shows that there is no contradiction between the Church's teaching on redemptive suffering and the need to relieve the suffering of our neighbor.

FURTHER STUDY

Catechism of the Catholic Church, §§272–274, 309–314.

Catholic Answers at Catholic.com

- Trent Horn, "Why Horrible Suffering Does Not Disprove God's Existence," August 21, 2015.

- Peter Kreeft, "The Problem of Suffering Reconsidered," March 1, 2002.

- Matt Nelson, "What is the Answer to Suffering?" February 14, 2018.

Peter Kreeft, *Making Sense Out of Suffering* (Ann Arbor, Michigan: Servant Publications, 1986).

Peter Kreeft and Ronald K. Tacelli, S.J., "The Problem of Evil," in *Handbook of Christian Apologetics: Hundreds of Answers to Crucial Questions* (Downers Grove, Illinois: InterVarsity Press, 1994), 120–146.

CHURCH AND SACRAMENTS

SALVATION

Can we be saved only through the Catholic Church?

Objection 1
Nowhere does Scripture indicate that one must be Catholic to be saved but rather that one must believe: "if you confess with your lips that Jesus is Lord and believe in your heart that God raised him from the dead, you will be saved" (Rom 10:9).

Objection 2
Many people are not born in a time or place or in a family where they can know Christ or the Church. It would be unfair to limit salvation by accidents of birth.

Objection 3
Since God is merciful, all or virtually all people go to heaven. The Church herself admits that she does not know all those who are in heaven. Scripture says that the will of God is for "all men to be saved and to come to the knowledge of the truth" (1 Tim 2:4). Thus it makes no sense to claim that there is no salvation outside the Church.

Objection 4
The Church has always taught that the prophets and patriarchs before Christ could be saved, and the Second Vatican Council admitted that even atheists can be saved. It is a contradiction then to state that one cannot be saved outside the Church.

Objection 5
The witness of holy non-Catholics and bad example of sinful Catholics suggests that limiting salvation to Catholics is unreasonable.

Objection 6
Stating that one cannot be saved outside the Church leads to fanaticism in Catholic missionary work.

CATHOLIC TEACHING

+ **Salvation is through Christ** since "there is no other name under heaven given among men by which we must be saved" (Acts 4:12). Jesus himself declares that "I am the way, and the truth, and the life; no one comes to the Father, but by me" (John 14:6).

+ **Christ founded a Church to continue his salvific work.** "The Church, in Christ, is like a sacrament—a sign and instrument, that is, of communion with God and of unity among all men."[1] All salvation comes from Christ the Head through the Church which is his Body.

+ **Christ and the Church, though not identical, are inseparable.** Taken together they constitute the "whole Christ"—an inseparability expressed in the New Testament by the analogy of the Church as Bride of Christ (see 2 Cor 11:2; Eph 5:25–29; Rev 21:2, 9).

+ **The Church is therefore necessary for salvation.** By stating the necessity of faith and baptism (see Mark 16:16; John 3:5), Jesus "affirmed at the same time the necessity of the Church which men enter through baptism as through a door."[2] Those who, knowing the Church to be divinely established by Christ, nevertheless refuse to enter or remain in her fold, cannot be saved.

+ **All the means of salvation are to be found in the Catholic Church.** Those outside her visible fold, writes Pope Pius XII, even if they have some relationship with the Mystical Body, "still remain deprived of those many heavenly gifts and helps which can only be enjoyed in the Catholic Church."[3]

+ **The Church exists to advance the salvation of all human beings.** Catholics have the privilege of bringing Christ and the means of salvation to all people. Every Mass is celebrated not just for Catholics but for all human beings. It is our role as Catholics not just generically to "get people to heaven" but to prepare

---

[1] *Lumen Gentium*, §1.

[2] *Lumen Gentium*, §14.

[3] Pope Pius XII, Encyclical on the Mystical Body of Christ *Mystici Corporis Christi*, June 29, 1943, §103.

people to live the kind of lives that prepare them for heaven.

+ **Those who are invincibly ignorant of the truth may still be saved.** "Those who, through no fault of their own, do not know the Gospel of Christ or his Church, but who nevertheless seek God with a sincere heart, and, moved by grace, try in their actions to do his will as they know it through the dictates of their conscience—those too may achieve eternal salvation."[4] As the Catechism teaches, "God has bound salvation to the Sacrament of Baptism, but he himself is not bound by his sacraments" (CCC §1257).

+ **Likewise, those who died before Christ could still be incorporated in Christ by faith** in his future coming, either by virtue of their good life or (in the case of the prophets) in their longing for the Savior.

REPLY

Reply to Objection 1: Scripture does not say that only Catholics can be saved.
We must believe in Christ in order to be saved, and this means that we must believe what he taught, including his establishment of the Church. We can hope for the salvation of non-Catholic Christians because outside the structure of the Church, there are elements of sanctification in ecclesial communities not in full communion with the Catholic Church. These elements, however, "derive their efficacy from the very fullness of grace and truth entrusted to the Catholic Church."[5] It therefore remains true that even non-Catholic Christians who are saved, are saved by virtue of the elements of sanctification found in the Catholic Church.

Reply to Objection 2 and 3: It would be unfair to limit salvation to Catholics; in any case, Scripture says all will be saved.
God does indeed will the salvation of all men and women and offers to each the possibility of choosing it in freedom, according to the circumstances of each. However, the grace of salvation, which every

---

[4] *Lumen Gentium*, §16.
[5] Second Vatican Council, Decree on Ecumenism *Unitatis Redintegratio*, November 21, 1964, §3.

person may receive, whether they know it or not, is the fruit of Christ's redemptive work mediated through his Body the Church. See *Can we really believe in eternal punishment for sinners?* (page 41) for a discussion about biblical teachings on heaven and hell.

Reply to Objection 4: The Church herself teaches that non-Catholics can be saved.
The Church teaches that the just souls who lived before Christ or those who are invincibly ignorant of the truth of Christ and the Church, may nonetheless reach salvation through the ministrations of Christ and his Church. Neither contradicts the teaching that all who are saved, are saved through the ministry of the Church that Jesus founded.

Reply to Objection 5: It is unreasonable to say that non-Catholics who are holy and virtuous cannot be saved.
Non-Catholics and even non-Christians can be saved by following God according to the lights they have received though their salvation is still effected through Christ and his Church. In fact, the objection simply highlights the greater responsibility Catholics have to become saints since they have received more clarity of the truth, more aids to salvation, and a clearer duty to pass on the gift of faith to others.

Reply to Objection 6: The idea that only Catholics can be saved leads to fanaticism.
Faith is a gift from God freely given and can only be freely received. It contradicts the very nature of faith to compel others to believe, which is the essential error of fanaticism. The Church's teaching, properly understood, can never lead to fanaticism.

FURTHER STUDY

Catechism of the Catholic Church, §§771–776, 839–856.

Catholic Answers at Catholic.com

- Jim Blackburn, "What 'No Salvation Outside the Church' Means," May 1, 2010.

- Fr. Ray Ryland, "No Salvation Outside the Church," December 1, 2005.

- Tim Staples, "Is There Really 'No Salvation Outside the Catholic Church?'" February 6, 2015.

- "What the Early Church Believed: Salvation Outside the Church," Tract, August 10, 2004.

Avery Cardinal Dulles, "Who Can Be Saved?" in *Catholic Controversies: Understanding Church Teachings and Events in History*, ed. Stephen Gabriel (Falls Church, Virginia: Moorings Press, 2010), 354–364.

Congregation for the Doctrine of the Faith, On the Unicity and Salvific Universality of Jesus Christ and the Church *Dominus Iesus*, August 6, 2000.

Peter Kreeft and Ronald K. Tacelli, S.J., "Salvation," in *Handbook of Christian Apologetics: Hundreds of Answers to Crucial Questions* (Downers Grove, Illinois: InterVarsity Press, 1994), 313–337.

COMMUNION

Why must one be Catholic to receive Holy Communion?

Objection 1
Excluding non-Catholics from the Eucharist is rude and condescending. In most other Christian churches, anyone can receive Communion whether or not he or she is a member. Jesus himself welcomed anyone who came to him and prayed that his followers "may all be one; even as you, Father, are in me, and I in you" (John 17:21). The Catholic insistence that someone be a member of their church to receive Communion is therefore contrary to the prayer of Jesus and divides his followers. It even erects barriers to conversion to the Catholic Church since people do not feel welcome at Mass.

Objection 2
In forbidding non-Catholics to receive Communion, the Catholic Church judges them to be unsuitable to receive the Eucharist. Yet Jesus said, "Judge not, that you be not judged" (Matt 7:1). Indeed there are many non-Catholics who live holier lives than many Catholics, and yet the former are prohibited from receiving Communion while the latter are welcomed.

Objection 3
Jesus said that "unless you eat the flesh of the Son of man and drink his blood, you have no life in you. . . . He who eats this bread will live forever." (John 6:53, 58). Barring non-Catholics from Communion means barring them from the source of eternal life.

Objection 4
The Catholic Church does allow, under certain conditions, baptized non-Catholics to receive the Eucharist. The fact that these Christians can receive Communion some of the time shows that they could receive it all the time.

Objection 5
The Catholic Church itself teaches that Eucharistic Communion unites believers. It "renews, strengthens, and deepens this incorporation into the Church, already achieved by Baptism" (CCC §1396). Communion is supposed be a source of unity, not a cause of further division.

CATHOLIC TEACHING

+ **Jesus revealed his True Presence in the Holy Eucharist** during his Bread of Life discourse. "I am the bread of life," he said, "the bread which comes down from heaven, that a man may eat of it and not die; . . . if any one eats of this bread, he will live forever; and the bread which I shall give for the life of the world is my flesh" (John 6:48–51). When questioned, Jesus emphasized again, "my flesh is food indeed, and my blood is drink indeed" (John 6:55; see CCC §1374).

+ **Such a gift as Jesus' own Body and Blood is held in the highest reverence** by the Catholic Church. The Second Vatican Council called it the "source and summit of the Christian life."[1] The Council also taught that the "other sacraments, and indeed all ecclesiastical ministries and works of the apostolate, are bound up with the Eucharist and are oriented toward it. For in the blessed Eucharist is contained the whole spiritual good of the Church, namely Christ himself."[2]

+ Communion unites us to Christ, renews the life of grace received at Baptism, cleanses us from venial sin, preserves us from future mortal sins, commits us to the poor, and is a sign and a source of unity with other members of the Church (see CCC §§1391–1397).

+ **Receiving Holy Communion is a profoundly sacred act, one that requires personal preparation** for so great and so holy a moment. St. Paul exhorts us to examine ourselves well. Whoever, he says, "eats the bread or drinks the cup of the Lord in an unworthy manner will be guilty of profaning the body and blood

---

[1] *Lumen Gentium*, §11.

[2] Second Vatican Council, Decree on the Ministry and Life of Priests *Presbyterorum Ordinis*, December 7, 1965, §5.

of the Lord. Let a man examine himself. . . . Anyone who eats and drinks without discerning the body eats and drinks judgment upon himself" (1 Cor 11:27–29). The Church teaches that any Catholic conscious of serious sin must go to Confession before receiving the Eucharist.

* **Receiving Holy Communion is not only a personal but also a public, ecclesial act. It is an expression of union with Christ and with his Church and with her teachings.** This is why the Eucharist is reserved to those in full communion with the Catholic Church. Under certain exceptional circumstances, such as the danger of death, a non-Catholic Christian can receive the Eucharist when he or she has the required dispositions and accepts the Catholic teaching regarding the Eucharist. Under ordinary circumstances, however, allowing non-Catholics to receive Communion would express an ecclesial unity that is not yet realized, and for which we must work and pray.

REPLY

Reply to Objection 1: Excluding non-Catholics from Communion is unwelcoming.

The Catholic Church understands herself to be the Mystical Body of Christ, not a merely human association. Being in union with the Church is therefore more than registering at a parish or being born into a Catholic family: it means being united to her teachings, to her sacramental life, and to her authority established "upon the foundation of the apostles and prophets" (Eph 2:20). Receiving Holy Communion is, then, not simply a personal act but a public act of communion with the Catholic Church as a whole. For this reason, she cannot admit to Holy Communion those who are not fully incorporated into her ecclesial life. This requirement is not intended to be divisive or unwelcoming or condescending. It is intended rather to be truthful about the lamentable state of disunity in the Church, and to encourage us all to work toward the unity for which Jesus prayed.

Reply to Objection 2: The Church is being judgmental in refusing Communion to non-Catholics.

Allowing only Catholics to receive Communion is not a judgment about anyone's faith or relationship with God. It does not repudiate the baptismal bond that Catholics share with other Christians nor deny that many non-Catholics live holier lives than many Catholics. It is, in fact, an affirmation that receiving Communion requires more than good personal dispositions; it also requires communion with the Church that Jesus founded. Simply being Catholic, it should be emphasized, is not enough either; Catholics must also examine their consciences and be in a proper state to receive worthily.

Reply to Objection 3: Barring non-Catholics from the Eucharist bars them from salvation.
God is able to save whomever he wills and is not limited by the sacraments, though those are the ordinary pathways through which he leads us to salvation. If someone is not able to receive the Eucharist, we ought not assume that they cannot be saved. Nevertheless, Jesus' words in the Bread of Life discourse are strong, and Catholics should do all they can to help others grasp the importance of being in full communion with the Catholic Church and receiving the Holy Eucharist.

Reply to Objection 4: Non-Catholics can receive in exceptional circumstances, so why not all the time?
The exceptional circumstances that allow for non-Catholics to receive Communion are just that: exceptional. In ordinary circumstances, the need for communion with the Church is not an arbitrary imposition but rather an honest assessment about the nature of Holy Communion and the ecclesial communion that it presupposes. Limiting Communion to Catholics respects both the holiness of the Blessed Sacrament and the dignity of each person's conscience.

Reply to Objection 5: The Eucharist is supposed to be a source of unity, not division.
It is true that Holy Communion is a "sign and sublime cause" for the "unity of the People of God" (CCC §1325). However, this unity is not simply that of communal harmony and fraternal charity. It is above all unity with God and with the Church as a whole, her teachings, and her hierarchical authority. It is a unity based upon revealed truth, in other words, that the Eucharist helps to promote, and for which we must also incessantly pray.

FURTHER STUDY

Catechism of the Catholic Church, §§1384–1405.

Catholic Answers at Catholic.com

+ "Who Can Receive Communion in the Catholic Church," Tract, August 10, 2004.

+ Kenneth Howell, "Why is Communion for Catholics Only?" February 1, 2003.

+ Jimmy Akin, "Conscience and Communion," October 20, 2015.

Pope John Paul II, On the Eucharist in its Relationship to the Church *Ecclesia de Eucharistia*, April 17, 2003.

Staff of Catholic Answers, "Who Can Receive Communion?" in *The Essential Catholic Survival Guide: Answers to Tough Questions About the Faith* (San Diego: Catholic Answers, 2005), 170–176.

CONFESSION

Why must I confess my sins to a priest?

Objection 1
Only God can forgive sins. The notion that a man can do so is blasphemous.

Objection 2
Jesus is the only mediator between God and human beings. "For there is one God, and there is one mediator between God and men, the man Christ Jesus" (1 Tim 2:5). Any Christian should therefore go directly to Jesus to have his or her sins forgiven.

Objection 3
If sins must be confessed to a priest, then non-Catholics cannot have their sins forgiven and hence cannot be saved. Since the Catholic Church teaches that non-Catholics can be saved, it is being inconsistent in requiring confession to a priest.

Objection 4
Confession to a priest was imposed by the Catholic Church in 1215 at the Fourth Lateran Council. It is neither scriptural nor apostolic.

Objection 5
Requiring the forgiveness of a priest gives him tremendous spiritual power, leading to clericalism and fostering abuse of clerical authority.

Objection 6
Hearing the sins of others will morally oblige a priest to act on some information that he receives in confession. For instance, he might learn of a penitent's criminal behavior, suicidal thoughts, or plans to harm another person. However, the Church forbids that he divulge or act on anything he hears. Thus confession places priests in a morally compromising position, and such cannot be the will of God.

CATHOLIC TEACHING

+ **Only God forgives sin.** Jesus, as the Son of God, does so repeatedly throughout the New Testament, as seen in the story of the paralytic, the penitent woman at the Pharisee's house, and the woman caught in adultery (see Matt 9:6–8; Luke 7:48; John 8:11).

+ **His ministry of reconciliation continues through the Church** which is "the sign and instrument of the forgiveness and reconciliation that he acquired for us at the price of his blood" (CCC §1442). He told his disciples at his Ascension "that repentance and forgiveness of sins should be preached in his name to all nations" (Luke 24:47). It is especially fitting that God who became man in Jesus Christ would wish to continue his ministry of mercy through his Body, the Church.

+ **After his Resurrection Jesus explicitly empowered his Apostles to forgive sins.** In the Upper Room he declared to them, "'As the Father has sent me, even so I send you.' And when he had said this, he breathed on them, and said to them, 'Receive the Holy Spirit. If you forgive the sins of any, they are forgiven; if you retain the sins of any, they are retained'" (John 20:21–23). In doing so, he confirmed his earlier promise to Peter that "whatever you bind on earth should be bound in heaven, and whatever you loose on earth shall be loosed in heaven" (Matt 16:19) and later expanded to all the Apostles (see Matt 18:18).

+ From her earliest days, the Church has understood the Apostles' authority to forgive sins as specific, not simply generic. That is, **they would absolve a person not of sin in general but of particular sins, which in turn implies the need to hear those sins in confession.** The Sacrament of Confession would parallel the Old Testament "guilt offering" for specific sins confessed to the priest, who "shall make atonement for him . . . and the sin which he has committed shall be forgiven him" (Lev 19:20–22).

+ **This power to forgive sins was not limited to the original Apostles,** as St. Paul affirms. "Christ reconciled us to himself," he writes to the Corinthians, "and gave us the ministry of reconciliation. . . . So we are ambassadors for Christ, God making his appeal through us. We beg you on behalf of Christ, be reconciled to God" (2 Cor 5:18–20; see also 2 Cor 2:10). St. James also refers to the power of priests to forgive sins (see Jas 5:14–16).

+ The Sacrament of Confession has changed over time, though it has kept the same fundamental structure through the centuries, namely "the acts of the man who undergoes conversion through the action of the Holy Spirit" and "God's action through the intervention of the Church" (CCC §1448).

+ **Confession must therefore always be accompanied by proper dispositions on the part of the penitent:** personal contrition, detestation for the sin, and the resolution not to sin again. Mortal sins must be confessed to a priest, though the Church teaches that perfect contrition—arising from the love of God above all else—"obtains forgiveness of mortal sins if it includes [in the case of Catholics] the firm resolution to have recourse to sacramental confession as soon as possible" (CCC §1452).

REPLY

Reply to Objection 1: Only God can forgive sins.
It is certainly true that only God forgive sins. Catholics confess their sins *to* God *through* a priest.

Reply to Objection 2: Christians should confess directly to Jesus, our sole mediator and priest.
There is indeed only one priest of the New Covenant: Jesus. And, as stated in the objection, we should ask forgiveness directly from God. After all, in the Lord's Prayer, we ask God (directly) to "forgive us our trespasses." The Sacrament of Confession contradicts neither truth. Though there is only one priest of the New Covenant, others do *participate* in his priesthood. Indeed, St. Peter teaches that all Christians participate in the common priesthood of the faithful (see 1 Pet 2:5). Catholics believe that there is another mode of participation, that of the ministerial priesthood, when priestly ordination configures a man to Christ as Head of the Church. In confessing our sins to a priest, then, we *are* confessing them to Jesus. Why would Jesus institute such a sacrament? There are many possible reasons. Through confession we are able to have a more personal encounter with the Lord. We hear the words of absolution and are assured of our forgiveness. We gain humility by acknowledging our sins. We receive grace to avoid sin in the future. We benefit from the priest's counsel. The simplest explanation for confessing our sins to a priest, however, is that

the Lord wills it. It is the means given by God to reconcile us to himself and to his Church, and we should gratefully accept this beautiful path of forgiveness rather than pridefully demanding another.

Reply to Objection 3: Then can only Catholics have their sins forgiven?
Confession is the ordinary path to reconciliation. However, non-Catholics (or Catholics who have no access to the Sacrament of Confession) can be forgiven with perfect contrition. The Church is therefore not being inconsistent in stating that non-Catholics also can be saved.

Reply to Objection 4: Confession is a later innovation of the Church.
The Fourth Lateran Council simply confirmed what had already been the age-old practice of the Church. Among the testimony of many ancient authorities, St. Hippolytus in the early 200s cites a prayer for the ordination of a bishop asking God to "let him have the power of high priesthood, to forgive sins according to your command."[1] As mentioned earlier, even Old Testament priests exercised a specific ministry of reconciliation for sinners.

Reply to Objection 5: Confession contributes to clericalism and the abuse of spiritual power.
The priest is a sinner himself, also in need of forgiveness through the ministry of another priest. He is simply an instrument of Christ's mercy. "The confessor is not the master of God's forgiveness, but its servant" (CCC §1466). If it contributes to clericalism, pride, or fosters abuse, that is not due to the nature of the ministry or the sacrament but rather to the priest's own sinful arrogance. The answer is not to repudiate the gift of the sacrament but to insist upon the holiness of its ministers.

Reply to Objection 6: Confession places priests in a morally compromising position.
Since the priest hears sins as an instrument of Jesus, not on his own authority, anything heard by the priest is not his to act on. While non-Catholics may consider this a quibble, it is of decisive importance to a believer who, with supernatural faith, sees beyond the merely human interaction to a genuine, personal encounter with God. The seal of the confessional is absolute because the privacy of the penitent's intimate encounter with God is absolute.

---

[1] St. Hippolytus, *On the Apostolic Tradition* in *St. Vladimir's Seminary Press Popular Patristics Series*, ed. John Behr, vol. 54, trans. Alistair C. Stewart (Yonkers, NY: St. Vladimir's Seminary Press, 2015), 73.

FURTHER STUDY

Catechism of the Catholic Church, §§1440–1470.

Catholic Answers at Catholic.com

- ✦ "What the Early Church Believed: Confession," Tract, August 10, 2004.

- ✦ Tim Staples, "Is Confession in Scripture?" March 28, 2014.

- ✦ Jason Evert, "How to Defend the Sacrament of Confession," October 1, 2001.

- ✦ Trent Horn, "God Chooses to Use Human Intermediaries," March 1, 2016.

Scott Hahn, *Lord Have Mercy: The Healing Power of Confession* (New York: Image, 2003).

Staff of Catholic Answers, "The Forgiveness of Sins," in *The Essential Catholic Survival Guide: Answers to Tough Questions About the Faith* (San Diego: Catholic Answers, 2005), 199–205.

William Saunders, "Why Go to Confession?" in *Catholic Controversies: Understanding Church Teachings and Events in History,* ed. Stephen Gabriel (Falls Church, Virginia: Moorings Press, 2010), 279–281.

Patrick Madrid, "Why Confess to a Priest?" in *Does the Bible Really Say That?: Discovering Catholic Teaching in Scripture* (Cincinnati: Servant, 2006), 44–47.

DIVORCE

Why can't Catholics get divorced?

Objection 1

Many marriages do not work out. Some are plagued by infidelity, bitter resentments, physical or emotional abuse, or a cooling of affection between the spouses. Children especially can find such conditions traumatic. Forbidding divorce in these cases is inhumane and unrealistic.

Objection 2

In forbidding divorce, Jesus himself made exceptions. "Whoever divorces his wife," he said, "*except for unchastity*, and marries another, commits adultery" (Matt 19:9). Since Jesus acknowledges that there are exceptions to the general rule, the Church can define what these exceptions are.

Objection 3

St. Paul allows for divorce when one of the partners is not baptized (the so-called Pauline privilege; see 1 Cor 7:10–15). The Orthodox churches allow divorce for a variety of reasons. Almost all Protestant churches allow for divorce. The Catholic Church alone holds an unreasonably strict view on divorce.

Objection 4

The Catholic solution to failed marriages is hypocritical because under the guise of being more faithful to the teaching of Jesus, the Church essentially permits "Catholic divorce" in its teaching on annulments. In addition, this solution renders children illegitimate since the Church is declaring that the marriage was invalid from the beginning.

CATHOLIC TEACHING

+ **Marriage is a community of love instituted by God himself.**
"The vocation to marriage is written in the very nature of man
and woman as they came from the hand of the Creator" (CCC
§1603). "Therefore a man leaves his father and his mother and
cleaves to his wife, and they become one flesh" (Gen 2:24). **Jesus,
moreover, instituted the Sacrament of Matrimony to imbue
the natural bond of marriage with a special grace** "to perfect
the couple's love and to strengthen their indissoluble unity"
(CCC §1641).

+ **Marriage cannot be dissolved by any human authority.** In the
Mosaic Law, divorce was permitted, but Jesus insists that "from
the beginning it was not so" (Matt 19:8). He then gives clear
instructions on the indissolubility of marriage. The man and
woman, he says, "are no longer two but one flesh. What therefore
God has joined together, let not man put asunder. . . . Whoever
divorces his wife and marries another, commits adultery against
her" (Mark 10:8–11 and parallels). The bond of marriage "gives
rise to a covenant guaranteed by God's fidelity. The Church
does not have the power to contravene this disposition of divine
wisdom" (CCC §1640).

+ **Reason as well as revelation demonstrates that marriage
is indissoluble** since it is a lifelong bond to which the spouses
freely consent and the most favorable environment for the caring
of children. Divorce introduces disorder into the family and into
society and often causes great turmoil in the lives of children.

+ **The exchange of consent between the spouses is the indispensable element of a marriage.** They must be capable of making
such a consent, and it must be free of coercion and grave fear.
**If the Church determines that such consent was not given or
could not be given, then the marriage never existed; this is
called a "declaration of nullity"** or an "annulment." A declaration of nullity can also be granted when the rite itself lacks
proper ecclesiastical form since sacramental marriage is a public
and liturgical act which creates rights and duties in the Church.

+ In cases where living together becomes extremely difficult or
even dangerous, couples may legitimately seek a separation.

There might even be reasons that justify a civil divorce, such as ensuring "certain legal rights, the care of the children, or the protection of inheritance" (CCC §2383). **Such legal recourse, however, should not be confused with a rupture of their union and does not free either party to remarry.**

+ Catholics who do remarry after civil divorce are in "a situation that objectively contravenes God's law" and cannot receive Holy Communion until they have "repented for having violated the sign of the covenant and of fidelity to Christ, and . . . are committed to living in complete continence" (CCC §1650; see also §2384).

REPLY

Reply to Objection 1: Forbidding divorce is inhumane and unrealistic.
The Church is being neither inhumane nor unrealistic in holding to the clear teaching of Jesus on divorce. The couple solemnly and freely vowed before God to remain united in marriage until death. The Catholic Church (and almost she alone) continues to take that sacred promise seriously. Moreover, tremendous damage is done to children, to society as a whole, and often to the couple themselves by the trauma of divorce.

Jesus has not placed on couples a burden impossible to bear. "By coming to restore the original order of creation disturbed by sin, he himself gives the strength and grace to live marriage in the new dimension of the Reign of God. It is by following Christ, renouncing themselves, and taking up their crosses that spouses will be able to 'receive' the original meaning of marriage and live it with the help of Christ" (CCC §1615). By closing off divorce as an option, the Church gives strength to couples and determination to work through difficulties rather than escaping from them.

Reply to Objection 2: Jesus himself stated that there are exceptions to the rule.
There is a great deal of debate surrounding the meaning of Jesus' words *"except for unchastity."* He might have been referring to marriages which were invalid due to consanguinity or other impediments. What is certain, however, is that he could not have been flatly contradicting the sentence itself, which reverses the Mosaic permissions for divorce. Also, if too much is read into the exception clause in St. Matthew's Gospel, then it contradicts the parallel passages (Luke

16:18 and Mark 10:6–12) as well as Pauline texts such as 1 Corinthians 7:10–15 and Romans 7:1–3. Scripture cannot contradict itself. Jesus' and Paul's clear teaching on marriage cannot be upended by one ambiguous clause. In the end, of course, it is the Church that must make the final determination about these texts, and the consistent teaching of the Church, from the very first centuries to the present day, has been unanimous and clear on the indissolubility of marriage.

Reply to Objection 3: St. Paul and other Christian churches allow for divorce. The Pauline privilege (derived from 1 Cor 7:10–15) permits divorce when an unbaptized spouse wishes to separate. This is an exception to the norm, granted in Scripture, for the good of both the baptized and the non-baptized person. It is important to note, however, that though these marriages can be valid, they are never sacramental since one of the spouses is not baptized. In this sense, the Pauline privilege does not constitute an exception to the teaching that valid and sacramental marriages can never be dissolved.

The teachings of other Christian churches vary widely. Suffice it to say that the teaching on the indissolubility of the marriage bond has been progressively weakened over the centuries in the Orthodox churches and, even more dramatically, in the Protestant communions. Comparing their teachings to virtually any ancient Christian authority, let alone the Scriptures, shows their drift from the original teaching of Christ.

Objection 4: Annulments are "Catholic divorce" and render children illegitimate.
Given the solemn vows pronounced by the couple at the time of their wedding, annulment is the only honest approach that legitimately permits a new marriage. It is not sanctimonious posturing or duplicitous "Catholic divorce"; it is a well-intentioned effort to find a way through a difficult situation so that the couple can know if they are married or not, and hence whether they are free to marry someone else.

In addition, a declaration of nullity does not render children illegitimate. Children born to parents who are married in good faith—who believe their marriage to be valid—are not rendered illegitimate by, for example, a defect in the parents' consent that is later discovered. Legitimacy, in any case, is a question of status before the law. Just as nothing changes in the children's status before civil law in the case of divorce (e.g., for the purposes of inheritance) so, too, does nothing change in the children's status before canon law in the case of annulment.

FURTHER STUDY

Catechism of the Catholic Church, §§1601–1658, 2382–2386.

Catholic Answers at Catholic.com

- ✦ Jim Blackburn, "Did Jesus Allow Divorce?" October 1, 2006.

- ✦ Leila Miller, "Eight Things You Have To Know About the Church's Teaching on Divorce," March 24, 2017.

- ✦ Jimmy Akin, "Divorce, Remarriage, and Communion," March 1, 2015.

- ✦ "What the Early Church Believed: Marriage," Tract, August 10, 2004.

- ✦ Rose Sweet, "Divorce, Annulment, Remarriage, and Communion: A Catholic Primer," July 5, 2018.

Robert Dodaro, *Remaining in the Truth of Christ: Marriage and Communion in the Catholic Church* (San Francisco: Ignatius Press, 2014).

Patrick Madrid, "Divorce and Remarriage," in *Does the Bible Really Say That?: Discovering Catholic Teaching in Scripture* (Cincinnati: Servant, 2006), 19–22.

ORDINATION

Why can't women be ordained priests?

Objection 1
Exclusion of women from the priesthood is unjust discrimination and relegates women to second-class status in the Church and, by extension, in society and the family. The male priesthood is sometimes defended by saying that priests must be men because Jesus was a man. This is an arbitrary standard, since priests obviously do not have to be, for example, Middle Eastern, or of a certain age, or of a particularly blood type. Thus reserving it to men alone is unreasonable and unfair.

Objection 2
Many women feel a call to the priesthood, and it is wrong to deny them ordination.

Objection 3
Ordination of women is good for the Church because women priests would alleviate a priest shortage, and many women can perform the functions of a priest better than many men.

Objection 4
The reason women are not ordained is because cultural norms prevented Jesus and the Apostles from ordaining women. If Jesus were alive today, he would have chosen some women apostles.

Objection 5
The early Church permitted deaconesses and/or priestesses, and hence so should we.

CATHOLIC TEACHING

+ **The Church is not free to ordain women**. Christ himself instituted the priesthood by choosing his Apostles from among men
only. The Church—including the pope—has no right or power
to act otherwise than her Lord. The question of whether to
ordain women, then, is not just a question of what the Church
ought to do; it is a question of what she *can* do. The Church has
repeatedly affirmed that she cannot ordain women because she
lacks the fundamental capacity and authority to do so.

+ **Christ's maleness reveals his relationship to humanity and the
Church**. The distinction of male and female is the only human
distinction willed by God (see Gen 1:27). Men and women both
image God equally but differently. The fact that Christ was a
male is, therefore, not a trivial characteristic. It does not indicate
any inherent superiority of men, but it does point to the uniquely
male characteristics of Jesus' redemptive mission.

+ Christ is the "New Adam" (as Mary is the "New Eve"), since **he
assumed in the order of grace the headship of the first Adam**.
That is, given the order of creation as it was constituted, only a man
could stand at the head of the entire human race to offer sacrifice as a
priest. It is this priesthood which Christ exercises that places him—
and the men who are configured to him through ordination—in a
spousal relationship with his feminine, receptive Bride, the Church.

+ **Equality is not sameness**. Catholics believe that men and women
are fundamentally equal in the dignity that they share as human
beings and as redeemed children of God. All the baptized, moreover, share in the one priesthood of Christ. This fundamental
equality is not undermined by meaningful differences of function and mission, however.

+ **Priesthood is not about power; it is about service**. Priests were
given their *mandatum*—the command of charity—at the Last
Supper when Jesus washed the feet of his Apostles. Humble
service, not worldly power and control, was to be the model
for priests of the Church. Many arguments for the ordination
of women stem from a view of human relationships based upon
power, not charity. Inasmuch as some priests have historically
failed to fulfill Christ's command and his example of love (indeed

none fulfill it perfectly), they are responsible for these erroneous standards of power associated with the priesthood.

+ **Mary was never ordained**. The greatest human creature, Mary, was not a priest. Clearly dignity—even the highest dignity—is not derived from ordination to the ministerial priesthood.

REPLY

Reply to Objection 1: Refusing to ordain women is a form of discrimination. Catholics believe that women and men are created with equal dignity. Human equality, however, does not mean identity. They have different, complementary roles (see Gen 1:26–27). This is not unjust discrimination but part of God's creation, strikingly visible in the naturally different roles of mothers and fathers. Masculinity and femininity are principles that reverberate throughout creation and redemption, and Jesus' own masculinity was an inseparable part of his Incarnation, his fatherhood in grace, and his spousal love for the Church. Since priests are conformed to Christ and exercise their spiritual fatherhood in union with the feminine Church, ordaining women would disregard and obscure the Church's femininity as the Bride of Christ. Additionally, implicit in this objection is the notion that the priesthood is a vocation of power and that female equality demands that women wield the same power. This claim misunderstands the very heart of the priesthood, which is a vocation of service to all the people of God.

Reply to Objection 2: Many women feel called to the priesthood.
This objection mistakes personal feelings for an objective vocation from God. A woman (or man) may desire the priesthood and have qualities well suited for priestly work and not have a vocation. The priesthood is not derived from the desire of the individual but a calling from God. No one has a right to the priesthood. Indeed, speaking more generally, not everything we desire is feasible or contributes to our goodness and holiness.

It should also be observed that women have an indispensable and irreplaceable role in the Church that priestly ordination would obscure. Together with all the faithful, but with the particular gifts which are theirs, women share in the priestly mission of Christ in their Christian witness and apostolate in the home, at work, and in charitable works. The noble desire of a woman to serve is fulfilled in her own unique vocation "according to the richness of the femininity which she received on the day of creation and which she inherits as an expression of the 'image and likeness of God' that is specifically hers"[1]—as holy women have done over the centuries.

Reply to Objection 3: Ordaining women would alleviate the priest shortage.
Even if the ordination of women would alleviate the shortage of priests, we can never ignore the will of the Lord for the sake of expediency. More importantly, the character of the priesthood is not reducible to external functions. The Sacrament of Holy Orders imparts an indelible character on the priest, conferring a special grace to serve as a representative of Christ, Head of the Church. This objection, then, relies on a false presupposition that anyone who can perform the *actions* of a priest is thereby qualified actually to *be* a priest.

Reply to Objection 4: Jesus didn't ordain women because it was against the cultural norms of his time.
Arguing that Jesus would be complicit in the cultural prejudice against women in his day, or ignorant of them, would mean that he is not the sinless Son of God. Moreover, Scripture is replete with examples of Christ's love and tenderness to women, including outcast women. This includes the Samaritan woman at the well (John 4:7–27) and the woman caught in adultery (John 8:3–11). "They marveled that he was talking to a woman" (John 4:27). Women stood at the foot of the cross (Matt 27:55; John 19:25), and women, not men, first found the empty tomb on Easter morning (Matt 28:1–10, Luke 24:8–11). Jesus' teaching and behavior demonstrate that he was not swayed by the discrimination against women prevalent in his day.

Reply to Objection 5: The early Church ordained women.
This assertion mischaracterizes the official role of women in the early Church. Since baptism was administered by full immersion, there were "deaconesses" (a Greek word simply meaning "female servants") who did not receive ordination but rather assisted in the rites of female catechumens. There were also official "orders" of consecrated virgins and widows. While some believe there were instances in history of women *acting* as priests, the practice was uniformly condemned as heretical by the Church. Then as now, abuse of the sacraments does not signal a change in the teaching and doctrine of the Church.

---

[1] St. John Paul II, Apostolic Letter On the Dignity and Vocation of Women *Mulieris Dignitatem*, August 15, 1988, §10.

FURTHER STUDY

Catechism of the Catholic Church, §§1577–1580.

Catholic Answers at Catholic.com

- Michael J. Tortolani, "Why No Women's Ordination?" January 1, 1996.

- "What the Early Church Believed: Woman and the Priesthood," Tract, August 10, 2004.

- Jason Evert, "Why Can't Women Be Priests?" January 1, 2002.

Pope John Paul II, Apostolic Letter on Reserving Priestly Ordination to Men Alone *Ordinatio Sacerdotalis*, May 22, 1994.

Joyce A. Little, "Ordination of Women," in *Catholic Controversies: Understanding Church Teachings and Events in History*, ed. Stephen Gabriel (Falls Church, Virginia: Moorings Press, 2010), 347–350.

Monica Migliorino Miller, *The Authority of Women in the Catholic Church* (Steubenville, Ohio: Emmaus Road Publishing, 2015).

Austen Ivereigh, "Women and the Church," in *How to Defend the Faith without Raising Your Voice: Civil Responses to Catholic Hot-Button Issues* (Huntington, Indiana: Our Sunday Visitor Publishing Division, 2012), 138–152.

Sara Butler, *The Catholic Priesthood and Women: A Guide to the Teaching of the Church* (Chicago: Hillenbrand Books, 2007).

PRIESTLY CELIBACY

Why must priests be celibate?

Objection 1
Celibacy discourages needed vocations to the priesthood. Many do not seriously discern a vocation to the priesthood because of the celibacy requirement. It should at least be optional.

Objection 2
St. Paul repeatedly assumes that clergy are married (see 1 Tim 3:2, 12; Titus 1:5–6). Thus, priestly celibacy is not scriptural.

Objection 3
Celibacy was imposed on Latin Rite priests in the twelfth century. Eastern Orthodox priests, who are generally married, represent an older and more authentic tradition in the Church.

Objection 4
Celibacy is inhuman and perhaps dangerous because it fosters sexual repression.

Objection 5
Celibacy is a relic of Old Testament ritual purity laws and the product of bad anthropology, which holds a dim view of human sexuality.

Objection 6
Celibacy is perceived as a "higher path" and reduces marriage to a second-class vocation in the Church.

CATHOLIC TEACHING

+ **Jesus was celibate,** as were many of his early disciples including St. Paul. Jesus extolled the value of celibacy "for the sake of the Kingdom of Heaven" as a gift. "Not all men can receive this precept, but only those to whom it is given" (Matt 19:11). Mary and Joseph did not exercise marital rights, and many of the early saints were extolled for their virginity.

+ **Celibacy has been valued by the Church from her very beginnings as a way of life that is especially conducive to contemplation and a heart undivided in its love for the Lord** (see 1 Cor 7:32–40). It is a gift to the Church of inestimable value, promoting a life of holiness and prayer.

+ Clerical celibacy fosters priestly spousality with the Church and opens priests to a deeper capacity for the exercise of spiritual fatherhood.[1] It enables the priest to more perfectly imitate the life and ministry of Jesus. It is also an eschatological sign of the kingdom to come (see Matt 22:30; Luke 20:35–36). "[A]ccepted with a joyous heart celibacy radiantly proclaims the Reign of God" (CCC §1579).

+ While celibacy is clearly not essential to the priesthood on one level (there are validly ordained priests who are married, even in the Latin Rite), nonetheless it should be noted that **the one Priest of the New Covenant, Jesus Christ, is himself celibate. In this sense, celibacy *is* inseparable from the priesthood** since all priests share in the one (celibate) priesthood of Jesus.

REPLY

Reply to Objection 1: Celibacy discourages priestly vocations.
Given the experience of non-Catholic Christian communities, it is by no means clear that abolishing celibacy would actually increase vocations to the priesthood in the long run. Even were that true, however, surrendering celibacy would forfeit supernatural gifts to the

---

[1] See *Presbyterorum Ordinis*, §16; Pope John Paul II, Post-Synodal Apostolic Exhortation *Pastores Dabo Vobis*, March 25, 1992, §29; and the author's *Why Celibacy?: Reclaiming the Fatherhood of the Priest* (Steubenville, OH: Emmaus Road, 2019).

Church of incalculable value since it is through celibacy that priests live a closer imitation of the ministry and life of Christ and a singular expression of ecclesial spousality, supernatural fatherhood, and eschatological witness. Even making celibacy optional would surrender many of these gifts since the natural tendency of human nature, especially in the current cultural climate, would likely lead to a dramatic reduction in those open to receiving the charism of celibacy. In addition, since it is almost certain that, as in the Eastern Churches, only celibate priests would be ordained bishops, it could promote a two-tier presbyterate of married and celibate priests, the latter able to become bishops. Those who remain celibate could even be perceived either as ambitious for clerical promotion or else unable or unwilling to be married.

Reply to Objection 2: Priestly celibacy is not scriptural.
St. Paul's insistence that a bishop be the "husband of one wife" (1 Tim 3:2) seems, at first glance, to be a clear refutation of clerical celibacy. However, Paul also insists that a *widow* receiving Church support be the "wife of one husband" (1 Tim 5:9). Clearly, since she is a widow, St. Paul can only mean that she has renounced any opportunity to marry again. St. Paul's statements about bishops and deacons likely refer to their renunciation of remarriage if they are (or become) widowed. In fact, it reinforces the historical claim that even in the very early Church, perpetual continence was the norm for priests, including those who were married at the time of their ordination. This was the Church's interpretation at least from the time of Pope Siricius (fourth century) until modern times. In any case, these texts of St. Paul do not contradict his other clear statements about the value of celibacy (1 Cor 7:7) or the celibate witness and teaching of Jesus himself (see Matt 19:11, 29; Matt 22:30). The notion that celibacy has no scriptural warrant, then, simply does not hold.

Reply to Objection 3: Priestly celibacy was imposed by the Church in the twelfth century.
Celibacy is of very ancient, even apostolic, origins. Though some of the Apostles were undoubtedly married, recent scholarship suggests that very early in the Church, married clergy lived marital continence (the *lex continentiae*). The practice of clerical celibacy grew rather than declined in the early centuries of the Church. The Council of Elvira (305) in Spain, for example, ratified what was already an ancient practice, obliging complete continence for clergy. Synods, local Councils, papal decrees, and even penitential books over the following centuries

did the same. The Second Lateran Council (1139) merely restated, in response to rampant abuses, what had long been the practice of the Latin Church and declared invalid any marriage contracted by a cleric. The Eastern Church did not hold as stringently to the apostolic norm, though even in the Eastern Churches, for whom the Council of Trullo (691) permitted temporary continence for married priests, ordination remained an impediment to marriage, and the celibate norm was (and still is) maintained for bishops who possess the fullness of Holy Orders.

Reply to Objection 4: Celibacy is unnatural and even dangerous since it leads to abusive behavior.
Celibacy, like marriage, is a vocation of love and, like marriage, must be lived well for it to be fruitful and healthy. When lived generously and supernaturally, celibacy is a profoundly satisfying way of life and a source of inestimable joy and apostolic effectiveness, as demonstrated by the witness of countless priests and religious through the centuries. Their testimony shows that sexual abuse is not caused by celibacy any more than adultery is caused by marriage. The source of clerical sexual abuse, in other words, is not celibacy; it is a lack of chastity.

Reply to Objection 5: Celibacy reflects an outdated anthropology that devalues sexuality.
Celibacy has admittedly been defended at times merely as the fulfillment of Old Testament ritual purity laws, and it has sometimes reflected a dim view of sexuality. But the Church's actual teaching about celibacy has always pointed to its greater spiritual openness, as St. Paul recommends even to married couples "by agreement for a season, that you may devote yourselves to prayer" (1 Cor 7:5). Official Catholic teaching has never proposed it as an implicit or explicit condemnation of sexual love itself.

Reply to Objection 6: Celibacy lowers marriage to second-class status in the Church.
St. Paul makes clear that marriage is a gift and a holy vocation, even as he speaks of the objectively greater excellence of celibacy (see 1 Cor 7:8–9, 32–38). That celibacy is so highly esteemed by the Church is an unspoken affirmation of the holiness of marriage, since only noble goods constitute a worthy sacrifice to God. Nevertheless, it must be admitted that the dignity and holiness of marriage, now strongly affirmed by the Church, has not always been fully appreciated even by many Catholic teachers.

FURTHER STUDY

Catechism of the Catholic Church, §§1579–1580.

Catholic Answers at Catholic.com

+ Jason Evert, "How to Argue for Priestly Celibacy," April 1, 2001.

+ "Celibacy and the Priesthood," Tract, August 10, 2004.

+ Greg Mockeridge, "Celibacy is a Gift," February 1, 2001.

+ Fr. Carter Griffin, "Why Celibacy?" October 25, 2019.

Carter Griffin, "The Beauty of Priestly Celibacy," *National Catholic Register*, June 24, 2019.

Carter Griffin, *Why Celibacy?: Reclaiming the Fatherhood of the Priest* (Steubenville, Ohio: Emmaus Road Publishing, 2019).

Pope Paul VI, Encyclical Letter On the Celibacy of the Priest *Sacerdotalis Caelibatus*, June 24, 1967.

Staff of Catholic Answers, "Celibacy and the Priesthood," in *The Essential Catholic Survival Guide: Answers to Tough Questions About the Faith* (San Diego: Catholic Answers, 2005), 192–198.

Thomas McGovern, *Priestly Celibacy Today* (Princeton: Scepter Publishers, 1998).

Stefan Heid, *Celibacy in the Early Church*, trans. Michael J. Miller (San Francisco: Ignatius Press, 1997).

PAPAL INFALLIBILITY

Is the pope really infallible?

Objection 1
There is no scriptural support for the idea that the pope is infallible.
It cannot be claimed as part of the Christian faith.

Objection 2
Christ's Church is comprised of many parts that together form one
Body. But the Catholic teaching that a single person can unilaterally
decide what every member of the faithful must believe is contrary to
this corporate unity. Therefore, the doctrine of papal infallibility is
contrary to the will of Christ.

Objection 3
The history of the Roman papacy is replete with scandal and corruption, showing that popes are men prone to sin and error. They
certainly are not infallible.

Objection 4
The doctrine of papal infallibility was not promulgated until 1870.
The teaching is not part of the original deposit of faith.

Objection 5
The first *ex cathedra* statement made by a pope claimed that the pope
enjoys the capacity to declare new doctrines *ex cathedra*. This is a circular argument and logically fails.

CATHOLIC TEACHING

+ **Christ left to his Church the authority to preach everything he taught** (see Matt 28:19–20) and promised that the Holy Spirit would "guide you into all truth" (John 16:13). The Church will never fall away from his teachings (see Matt 16:18) since it is "the Church of the living God, the pillar and bulwark of the truth" (1 Tim 3:15) even if individual Christians or Christian communities drift from the truth.

+ **Jesus entrusted leadership of his Church to the Apostles** who, whatever their personal failings, would be guided infallibly by the Holy Spirit in their teaching office. They understood themselves to have this authority, as is evident from the Council of Jerusalem when they wrote to the Gentiles certain instructions that "seemed good to the Holy Spirit and to us" (Acts 15:28).

+ As successors of the Apostles, **the College of Bishops as a whole is infallible when teaching a matter of faith or morals in union with the pope.** Jesus said, "He who hears you hears me" (Luke 10:16), and "[w]hatever you bind on earth shall be bound in heaven" (Matt 18:18). This Apostolic Tradition, safeguarded by the Holy Spirit, has preserved intact the divine deposit of faith entrusted to the Church and has guided its authentic development through the centuries.

+ **St. Peter was the head of the College of Apostles** (see Matt 16:17–19) as the pope is head of the College of Bishops. The pope enjoys the same infallibility as the College of Bishops "when, as supreme pastor and teacher of all the faithful—who confirms his brethren in the faith—he proclaims by a definitive act a doctrine pertaining to faith or morals."[1] This is known as teaching *ex cathedra*, from the Chair of Peter.

+ **The pope does not "invent" any teachings.** The deposit of faith is the Gospel itself, the teachings revealed by Jesus and conveyed by his Apostles. Public revelation ended with the death of the last Apostle. The role of the Church's teaching office is to protect it from error and to ensure that any new teachings are genuine developments of the original deposit of faith. The College

---

[1] *Lumen Gentium*, §25. See CCC §891.

of Bishops in an ordinary way, and the pope in an extraordinary way, do so through a special gift of the Holy Spirit.

- **The pope does not exercise this gift unilaterally.** Rather, he clarifies or defines, in fidelity to Christ's teaching and only in conformity with Scripture, the Tradition and the Church's Magisterium, what the Church has believed and lived from her beginning.

REPLY

Reply to Objection 1: There is no scriptural support for papal infallibility. The witness both of Scripture and Tradition support papal infallibility. Christ named Peter Cephas (John 1:42)—meaning rock or stone—and told him that he would be the rock upon which his Church was to be built, entrusting the keys of the kingdom to him. "I will give you the keys of the kingdom of heaven," Jesus told him, "and whatever you bind on earth shall be bound in heaven, and whatever you loose on earth shall be loosed in heaven" (Matt 16:19). This is a clear reference to the steward of the royal household in ancient Israel (see Isa 22:20–22) who exercised the authority of his master. Christ later enjoins Peter to strengthen the faith of the other Apostles (see Luke 22:32) and to act as shepherd in his stead (see John 21:15–17). St. Paul also refers to Cephas as an authoritative apostolic figure to whom dispute and disagreements are brought for adjudication and resolution (see Gal 2:7–14). Peter's authority is also demonstrated in various passages in the Acts of the Apostles. Most importantly, Scripture itself, canonized and promulgated by the Church, cannot be read independently of that same Church as its interpretive mechanism. Ultimately it is the authority of the Church that affirms the doctrinal primacy of the pope and his charism of infallibility.

Reply to Objection 2: Papal infallibility promotes a unilateral exercise of power.
The pope cannot invent any new teachings. Rather, he gives more definitive expression to the content of the deposit of faith, which was entrusted to the Apostles and their successors to interpret and develop through divine assistance. Moreover, papal infallibility is a negative charism, protecting his *ex cathedra* statements from error; it is neither a replacement for his theological study and collaboration nor a guarantee that he will positively teach all that he should.

Reply to Objection 3: The history of corrupt popes shows that they could not be infallible.

Though "corrupt popes" were less common than many polemical works suggest, it is evident from history that the pope is neither impeccable (incapable of sin) nor inerrant (incapable of error). This in no way undercuts the dogmatic proclamation of the pope's ability to teach infallibly *ex cathedra*. Whatever the imperfections of the man who occupies Peter's See, the supernatural protection from error holds true for the definitive clarification of matters concerning faith and morals. It does not preserve him from error in rendering judgments on customs, discipline, Church law, or even his personal theological positions that are not taught in a definitive way. In fact, it is remarkable that despite their sinfulness, even the "bad popes" never changed Church teachings to suit their personal interests. The few cases normally brought up in opposition to papal infallibility, including Paul's rebuke of Peter for refusing to eat with Gentile Christians or Pope Honorius' purported defense of Monothelitism, are personal errors, errors regarding discipline, or clearly do not meet the requirements of papal *ex cathedra* statements.

Reply to Objection 4: The doctrine of papal infallibility is a recent development.

Papal infallibility is not an innovation. Various ecumenical councils through the centuries have affirmed the primacy of the See of Rome, including the primacy of its teaching office, as did many Church Fathers. Early popes, too, were clearly aware of their teaching primacy and their duty to "confirm the brethren." What is new is not the notion of infallibility but rather the more precise articulation of the doctrine and the conditions for its exercise at the First Vatican Council.

Reply to Objection 5: The pope "infallibly" teaches about his own infallibility.

Just as the pope by speaking *ex cathedra* clarifies, solidifies, or explains new insights into the deposit of faith or necessary truths that devolve from it, so, too, is the First Vatican Council's 1870 teaching on papal infallibility a solidification and formulation of what the Tradition already believed from the beginning of Christianity. Its affirmation of the pope's charism of infallibility is not, therefore, an exercise in circular reasoning.

FURTHER STUDY

Catechism of the Catholic Church, §§888–892.

Catholic Answers at Catholic.com

- ◆ "Papal Infallibility," Tract, August 10, 2004.

- ◆ Jason Evert, "How to Argue for Papal Infallibility," February 1, 2002.

- ◆ Jimmy Akin, "Identifying Infallible Statements," September 1, 2001.

First Vatican Council, Dogmatic Constitution on the Church of Christ *Pastor Aeternus*, July 18, 1870.

Staff of Catholic Answers, "Papal Infallibility," in *The Essential Catholic Survival Guide: Answers to Tough Questions About the Faith* (San Diego: Catholic Answers, 2005), 48–54.

Catholics United for the Faith, "Pillar and Bulwark of the Truth: The Infallible Magisterium of the Catholic Church," in *Catholic Controversies: Understanding Church Teachings and Events in History*, ed. Stephen Gabriel (Falls Church, Virginia: Moorings Press, 2010), 314–321.

SOLA SCRIPTURA

Is Scripture the only rule of faith?

Objection 1
The Bible teaches that it alone is the rule of faith, that "all Scripture is inspired by God . . . that the man of God may be complete, equipped for every good work" (2 Tim 3:16–17). If Scripture is ordered to the "completeness" of man, then it is sufficient for salvation. While Christians differ on teachings in the Bible, the main message—what is needed for salvation and living according to the will of God—is abundantly clear. It is presumptuous and illogical to claim that we need the uninspired teachings of a church to understand the inspired teachings of the Bible.

Objection 2
It is true that initially the Apostles taught orally, but with the close of the apostolic age, all revelation that God wanted transmitted to human beings was articulated in the Scriptures. Reformers simply restored this ancient understanding to the Church.

Objection 3
The early Church Fathers all taught and defended Christianity against heresies with the sole authority of Scripture.

Objection 4
God would not have left succeeding generations to sift through extra-biblical revelation that was necessary for their salvation.

Objection 5
The Bible constantly warns us "not to go beyond what is written" (1 Cor 4:6). Moses told this to the Israelites (Deut 4:2) and Solomon repeated it in Proverbs (Prov 30:5–6). John says it again at the end of the Bible (Rev 22:18–19). Thus the Bible affirms that one should not seek for revelation outside the Bible.

Objection 6
The Catholic is guilty of circular reasoning. The Church, he says, is infallible because the Scriptures say so, and Scripture is infallible because the Church says so.

CATHOLIC TEACHING

+ Christ commanded his Apostles to preach the Gospel and "communicate the gifts of God to all men" (CCC §75). This commission continued in the bishops that the Apostles left as their successors.

+ The first spreading of the Gospel was oral through the preaching of the Apostles: "Go therefore and make disciples of all nations . . . teaching them to observe all that I have commanded you" (Matt 28:19–20. See also 2 Thess 2:15; 1 Cor 11:2). **This oral transmission of the Gospel is called Tradition. Under the inspiration of the Holy Spirit, the Gospel was also committed to writing, and this is called Sacred Scripture.**

+ **These two modes of transmission, Tradition and Sacred Scripture, emerge from the same divine source: Jesus.** "Each of them makes present and fruitful in the Church the mystery of Christ" (CCC §80) and both are to be honored with equal devotion. No interpretation of Scripture that contradicts Tradition is valid, and Tradition is never in contradiction with Sacred Scripture.

+ **Scripture itself affirms the need for an authoritative interpreter** (see 2 Pet 1:20–21). As the Ethiopian eunuch asks the deacon St. Philip, "How can I [understand], unless some one guides me?" (Acts 8:26–40). The authority instituted by Christ to teach in his name, including the interpretation of the Scriptures, is found precisely in the Magisterium (or teaching office) of the Church he founded (see Matt 16:13–20; Luke 10:16; Eph 2:20).

+ St. Paul calls the Church (not Scripture) the "pillar and bulwark of the truth" (1 Tim 3:15). The Protestant view of the Church as an invisible entity of believers united in faith cannot be this "pillar" since it is laden with deep doctrinal differences. Moreover it is clear that **the Apostles themselves understood that this visible entity would endure beyond their own deaths,** as shown in the election of Matthias who "was enrolled with the eleven apostles" (Acts 1:26), the episcopal ordinations of St. Timothy and St. Titus, and the ordination of the first seven deacons.

+ **The very content of the Scriptures is dependent upon the authority of the Church.** Without the Church's identification of the canon of the Bible, it is impossible to know which books are inspired and which copies faithfully transmit those original, inspired texts.

REPLY

Reply to Objection 1: The Bible itself teaches sola Scriptura.
St. Paul writing that "all Scripture is inspired by God . . . that the man of God may be complete" (2 Tim 3:16–17) does not prove that Scripture is the sole rule of faith. First, it is talking about the Old Testament (the Scriptures from Timothy's "childhood"), so if Protestants are correct, it proves too much. It would mean that the New Testament was either not inspired or not needed for the man of God to be "complete." Second, it says that Scripture is inspired and necessary, which is certainly true, but never does it say it is sufficient. Many things (like water) are necessary for life and yet not sufficient.

More broadly, it is simply not true that Protestants agree on central tenets of the faith clearly enunciated in the Bible. The divine essence of the Persons of the Trinity, the two wills in Christ, the hypostatic union, the cessation of revelation upon the death of the last Apostle, the canon of Scripture, infant Baptism, the regenerative power of Baptism, and the nature of the Eucharist are only a few of these core teachings upon which "Biblical" Christians disagree. It is not possible that Jesus intended such doctrinal confusion to reign in his Church; in fact, he explicitly stated otherwise. Ultimately *sola Scriptura* makes each person his own authoritative interpreter, causing doctrinal division and disunity and endangering souls. God would not have given us a Bible without the means to interpret it.

Reply to Objection 2: Revelation closed with the death of the last Apostle; thus there is no Sacred Tradition.
Public revelation did indeed conclude with the death of the last Apostle, but the transmission and interpretation of that revelation have continued through the centuries by Sacred Tradition.

Reply to Objection 3: The Church Fathers relied only on the authority of Scripture.
Scripture was never regarded or used by Church Fathers as something standing alone, self-sufficient and independent of Sacred Tradition and the Magisterium, the "living, teaching office of the Church" which is "not superior to the Word of God, but is its servant" (CCC §§85–86). The Church Fathers had a profound love and reverence for the Scriptures, but selective quotations ignore their forceful teachings on the necessary role and teaching of the Church.

Reply to Objection 4: Requiring more than the Bible would be unfair to Christians seeking salvation.
The argument works in the other direction. It is true that God would not leave Christians ignorant of important revelations, and that is precisely why Jesus founded his Church. The notion that Scripture alone is the authority for Christian teaching is an historical novelty begun in the fourteenth century by John Wycliffe. It is inconceivable that for thirteen centuries God would have left Christians so vulnerable to error unless they were fortunate enough to be literate and own a hand-copied Bible. God did not leave the vast majority of his people to rely on the invention of the printing press and inexpensive Bibles in order to receive a saving knowledge of his Son.

Reply to Objection 5: The Bible warns against going beyond the Scriptures.
These arguments are not logical. Moses told the Israelites, "You shall not add to the word which I command you, nor take from it" (Deut 4:2). Taken literally, that would mean that all Scriptures written afterwards—including most of the Old Testament and the whole New Testament—would be uninspired and illegitimate. All these passages simply forbid changes to the words or the meaning of those individual books. To assert otherwise is to do violence to the text and distort its plain meaning.

Reply to Objection 6: The Catholic teaching is circular reasoning.
The Church is not infallible because the Scriptures say so but because Jesus says so.[1] Our faith in the reliability of the Scriptures begins by examining their historical authenticity, which in turn allows us to evaluate the authority of the Church. It is that authority which gives us confidence in the inspiration of the Scriptures. The authority of

---

[1] See Tim Staples, "According to Scripture," in *Catholic Answers* (January 1, 2007) for a fuller response to the "circular reasoning" objection.

the Church is further reinforced by the witness of sanctity through the centuries, miracles, and other motives of credibility.

FURTHER STUDY

Catechism of the Catholic Church, §§75–95.

Catholic Answers at Catholic.com

+ Jimmy Akin, "What Exactly Do You Mean by Sola Scriptura?" July 1, 2005.

+ Kenneth Hensley, "Why I'm Catholic: The Foundational Error of Sola Scriptura," August 29, 2016.

+ Kenneth Hensley, "Why I'm Catholic: Sola Scriptura Isn't Scriptural" (4 parts), September 6, 2016.

+ Dave Armstrong, "A Quick Ten-Step Refutation of Sola Scriptura," September 1, 2004.

+ Dave Armstrong, "Ten Deficiencies of Sola Scriptura as a Rule of Faith," May 1, 2012.

+ Mark A. McNeil, "Another Look at Sola Scriptura's Best Defense," December 3, 2018.

Staff of Catholic Answers, "Proving Inspiration," in *The Essential Catholic Survival Guide: Answers to Tough Questions About the Faith* (San Diego: Catholic Answers, 2005), 63–69.

Patrick Madrid, "Scripture Alone?" in *Answer Me This!* (Huntington, Indiana: Our Sunday Visitor Publishing Division, 2003), 37–63.

MORALITY

ABORTION

Why does the Church teach that abortion is wrong and should be illegal?

Objection 1

Abortion is morally permissible since a fetus is not yet a complete human being. It is either a part of the mother's body and hence not a separate individual, or else—even if it is considered a separate individual—it is neither viable on its own nor can it exhibit personal actions such as reasoning and loving. Thus it should not be accorded the same rights as human beings who are already born.

Objection 2

The status of the fetus is ambiguous, so it is better to err on the side of the mother's reproductive rights, including legal access to abortion.

Objection 3

An unwanted child can diminish the potential life of the mother by limiting her freedom and causing mental stress. In these cases, abortion is justified due to the burdens imposed by the child and responsibilities of unwanted motherhood; it is analogous to self-defense against an unjust aggressor.

Objection 4

It is better to abort a fetus than to bring a child into the world who is undesired or who is expected to have a low quality of life for economic, mental, or physical reasons. This is especially true today in light of overpopulation concerns and environmental sustainability.

Objection 5

One can personally believe that abortion is wrong and still think that it ought to be legal since it is unjust to impose our morality on others. Even if abortion were illegal in most circumstances, there are exceptional circumstances that certainly justify it, such as rape, incest, or grave threats to the health of the mother.

CATHOLIC TEACHING

+ **Life begins at conception.** A new life comes into being at the time of conception, with a particular genetic combination, distinct from both mother and father, which has never before existed and will never be repeated. There is no question that it is human life; the fetus will only grow into a more developed human, never into a dog or a monkey. Moreover, reason demonstrates that conception is the only philosophically tenable beginning of a new human life. Attempts to demarcate a different "beginning" of human life in order to justify abortion necessarily depend upon arbitrary criteria, such as implantation, absence of a potential for twinning, development of a primitive streak, brain activity, the second trimester, viability, or the moment of birth. This is why, from "the first moment of his existence, a human being must be recognized as having the rights of a person" (CCC §2270).

+ **Human beings enjoy a dignity and a right to live, by their very nature.** It does not depend on our intelligence or talents, on our physical characteristics, on our degree of social usefulness, or whether or not we happen to have been born yet.

+ **Our right to live is not bound to a certain "quality of life."** Every human person is made in the image and likeness of God and is intrinsically valuable, whether or not his or her personal characteristics or anticipated family environment predict a sufficient "quality of life." No one has the authority to decide which lives are worth protecting and which can be discarded. Such logic leads inevitably to a eugenic mentality and ultimately endangers not only the unborn but the elderly, the sick, the disabled, and others with special needs.

+ **Destroying innocent human lives is an offense against God who is the author of life.** It is also a grave injustice to the dignity of the individual and threatens the social order since it threatens the legal protection of other human lives.

+ **One of the fundamental aims of law is to protect innocent human life.** It is never justified to intentionally kill innocent human life. Even in the difficult cases of a child conceived through rape or incest, it is still not right to destroy the unborn baby. The baby did not commit the crime. It would be responding to one great wrong with another great wrong.

+ **The Catholic teaching is not only anti-abortion; it is pro-life and pro-woman.** Abortion is a tragedy for the child, of course, but also for the mother. As Catholics we are determined not only to protect the unborn but also to help women who courageously carry a child to term, particularly in the face of personal anxiety and fear, resistance from others, or the threat of social rejection.

REPLY

Reply to Objection 1: The fetus is not human, or at least not a person.
Each of these arguments presumes that a real distinction can be made between a human life and a human person. There is simply no doubt scientifically that a fetus is a unique, separate, human organism. It is incoherent to argue that a woman carrying a genetically-distinct male fetus, for instance, is simply growing another part of her body. It is true, of course, that many functions we associate with human beings, such as the use of reason, are not exercised by a fetus, but it also true that those capacities exist in (and only in) the human fetus. Trying to identify when someone achieves "personhood," based upon "viability" or external characteristics or abilities, becomes a highly subjective— and ultimately dangerous—endeavor. It is a short road to the cruel mentality of eugenics. If the unborn can be excluded from the legal protections due to persons, so can any other category of human beings deemed unfit or unwanted.

Reply to Objection 2: The status of a fetus is ambiguous.
Ambiguity about the fetus would be an argument against abortion, not for it. The unintentional killing of someone through reckless behavior is considered manslaughter. If someone is hunting and hears a rustling in the bushes, he should refrain from shooting at the noise since he might inadvertently shoot his hunting companion. Ignorance demands restraint particularly when there are lethal repercussions, as in the case of abortion.

Reply to Objection 3: An unborn baby can pose a threat to the mother's well-being.
Many pregnant women experience anguish and fear at the prospect of bringing a child into the world. Catholics must stand ready to provide encouragement, clarity, and material and emotional support to

women in crisis pregnancies and to continue that support after birth. Nevertheless, intentionally killing an innocent human being is never the answer. If one's personal preferences, however strongly felt, eclipse the right of another person to live, then the rule of law succumbs to the notion that "might makes right." The legal basis of civilization would have no foundation. In such a society, no one can presume upon the protection of law.

The argument that abortion is a matter of self-defense because the child would impose severe emotional, financial, or social strain on the mother is likewise untenable. Killing in self-defense presumes a direct and immediate threat to one's own life or someone else's, not the threat of economic, social, or emotional difficulties.

Reply to Objections 4: Abortion is better than a baby being born unwanted or with a low quality of life.
It is never an act of mercy to destroy an innocent human being, however "unwanted" he or she is, and however diminished one judges his or her future quality of life to be. If abortion is wrong, then it is never justified by stating that the "ends justify the means." Moreover, even within the narrow logic of this objection, abortion sacrifices countless human possibilities. How many contributions to humanity—in science, the arts, medical advances, leadership—have already been lost by the millions of abortions that have occurred in the United States alone since 1973?

Reply to Objection 5: Abortion is wrong, but I should not impose my morality on others; or abortion should be legal at least some of the time.
If abortion is the intentional taking of innocent human life, we have an obligation to defend human life through custom and law, and no good intentions, no difficult circumstances, can justify it. Those who are hesitant to defend legal protection for the unborn either do not understand the gravity of abortion or lack the will and the courage to defend innocent human lives. In certain cases, when the health of the mother is in grave danger, medical intervention may be permissible even though a regrettable side-effect of the treatment may be the death of the unborn child. This, however, is very different from deliberate abortion.

FURTHER STUDY

Catechism of the Catholic Church, §§2270–2275.

Catholic Answers at Catholic.com

+ "What the Early Church Believed: Abortion," Tract, August 10, 2004.

+ Trent Horn, "Answering the Back-Alley-Abortion Objection," May 28, 2019.

Austen Ivereigh, "Defending the Unborn," in *How to Defend the Faith without Raising Your Voice: Civil Responses to Catholic Hot-Button Issues* (Huntington, Indiana: Our Sunday Visitor Publishing Division, 2012), 91–106.

Patrick Madrid, "Abortion," in *Where is That in the Bible?* (Huntington, Indiana: Our Sunday Visitor Publishing Division, 2001), 144–145.

Michael Baruzzini, "Why Conception?" in *Catholic Controversies: Understanding Church Teachings and Events in History*, ed. Stephen Gabriel (Falls Church, Virginia: Moorings Press, 2010), 453–456.

ASSISTED SUICIDE

Why does the Church prohibit assisted suicide?

Objection 1
People have the right to do with their own bodies what they wish without interference from state or religious power. If someone is suffering and wishes to end his or her life, nobody has the right to stand in the way.

Objection 2
People have a right to a "death with dignity." Today, many live longer lives but often accompanied by a loss of physical and intellectual capacities, a sense of diminished personal worth, and a feeling that they have become a burden to others. We euthanize our animals when they are severely hurt or in pain; how much more should we allow humans to choose death when they, all the more acutely, experience intense pain?

Objection 3
Medical costs continue to soar, driven in part by the costs of treating people for longer than they often wish to live. Assisted suicide is both more dignified and more economical, preserving resources for those in greater need.

Objection 4
The Church already permits removing life support when someone is near the end of his or her life or giving morphine to someone in intense pain even if these actions will lead to the patient's death. The Church even permits someone to sacrifice his or her life in order to save the lives of others. In other words, in certain cases, causing one's own death is permitted, and hence assisted suicide can at times be ethically justified.

CATHOLIC TEACHING

+ Moved with compassion, many in the assisted suicide movement laudably wish to free people from intense pain. The dying are often neglected and receive inadequate pain relief. We need to **respect and cherish our sick and elderly,** especially when they are suffering or dying.

+ Nevertheless, it is **never permitted to take innocent human life.** Assisted suicide violates this divine law, and hence no human power has the authority to sanction it. While the subjective guilt of those who commit suicide may be greatly diminished because of fear, depression, or mental illness (see CCC §2282), a medical professional assisting someone *else* in taking his or her own life may be committing an even graver fault. It is a deliberate act which, despite the good intentions, intends the death of the most vulnerable: the ill, the elderly, and the disabled. Vulnerable individuals deserve more, not less, support, compassion, and legal protection.

+ For the Christian, suffering can be endowed with meaning and purpose when united to Christ (see Col 1:24), and dying is the process of detachment and abandonment which prepares us for eternal life. Nevertheless, the Church's opposition to assisted suicide rests **not on revelation but the claim, through reason alone, that it is contrary to the common good.**

+ There are two main reasons for this claim. First, **if helping someone to end his or her life is legal, then the legal protection of all human life is weakened.** The line between "assisting someone to die" and murder can, in many circumstances, be less than clear. If the law authorizes death as a medical treatment, if helping someone commit suicide is ethically permissible or even praiseworthy, then "confining it to the dying seems arbitrary at best."[1] Indeed, in Belgium, where physician-assisted suicide is legal, *children* are now assisted in their desire to end their lives when they experience "unbearable suffering." There is no age restriction; as of this writing, the youngest child to be euthanized was only nine years old.

---

[1]   Austen Ivereigh, *How to Defend the Faith without Raising Your Voice* (Huntington, IN: Our Sunday Visitor, 2012), 63. I am grateful for Ivereigh's insights on this topic, many of which are woven into this discussion.

+ The second reason why assisted suicide is contrary to the common good is that it **will inevitably increase pressure on individuals to commit suicide.** Many elderly and sick people already feel that they are a burden to others and will feel it more acutely when they, in the new paradigm, "choose not to die." Deciding to allow nature to take its course will increasingly come to be seen as unusual and even selfish. **Prohibiting assisted suicide helps protect the elderly, the terminally ill, the depressed, and other vulnerable people** from ending their lives for fear of being a financial or emotional burden to others.

REPLY

Reply to Objection 1: People can do what they want with their bodies.
Personal autonomy is a great good, but it is not the only good. After all, our actions have an impact on others around us, particularly actions as weighty as suicide. Even if personal autonomy were the ultimate goal, it is not at all clear that assisted suicide promotes it. Evidence from jurisdictions where assisted suicide has been legal for some time suggest that life-ending decisions are often made based on erroneous prognoses or when clinically depressed. Is making the decision to end one's life, often with inaccurate information, when one is old, sick, and fearful, frequently alone and isolated at home, weeks or months after receiving the lethal prescription, really a true expression of "personal autonomy"?

Reply to Objection 2: People have a right to death with dignity.
Those who see no value in suffering, for whom every indignity associated with growing old and sick must be avoided at all costs, may not be convinced by any argument against assisted suicide. However, many people recognize that our self-worth should not be—and is not—wrapped up in our productivity, in our human capacities, and in our perceived "dignity." As the objection itself points out, we euthanize our animals when they are defective or in pain; assisted suicide suggests that some human beings can, like animals, be dispensed with because their lives are not deemed worthy or dignified enough. Once we class certain human beings as lacking sufficient "dignity" or quality of life, even if people make that judgment about themselves, then anyone can ultimately be classed as lacking sufficient dignity to live.

Reply to Objection 3: Assisted suicide saves valuable medical dollars and resources.

Assisting people to commit suicide whose medical care is allegedly too expensive establishes a dangerous precedent. It authorizes a lethal prescription that is often much cheaper than life-prolonging options. This dynamic invariably threatens society's most vulnerable populations, particularly the sick and the elderly. Moreover, the Church does not require that all treatments, no matter how expensive, must be pursued. Only "ordinary" treatments that are well established, proven, and not excessively burdensome are obligatory. "Extraordinary" treatments—those that are experimental, carry serious physical or psychological side effects, or are prohibitively expensive—may be omitted in making decisions about medical care.

Reply to Objection 4: The Church already authorizes suicide in certain cases.
The cases proposed in the objection do not constitute examples of the Church authorizing assisted suicide. Removing devices that assist breathing or kidney or liver functions when end of life is imminent does not cause death; it simply allows the process of dying to take place because it can no longer be prevented. A decision at the end of someone's life is not the same thing as a decision that *ends* someone's life. This is not a mere play on words; it is the difference between killing someone and allowing an unpreventable natural death to take its course.

Foregoing extraordinary treatments does not cause death but rather omits medical interventions that are out of proportion to the benefits received. Moreover, giving high doses of morphine, when the degree of pain calls for it, does not "speed up" the process of dying. In fact, sometimes it lengthens life by moderating pain and rendering patients more comfortable. If the purpose is to ease pain and no more is used than needed, these medications have as their end the relief of pain, not death.

Finally, sacrificing oneself to save others is not done in order to die; it is done in order that others may live. A soldier jumping on a hand grenade to save his platoon is not choosing to die; he is choosing the only option available to save the others. If there were another obvious route for him to take, he would do so.

None of these cases, then, are analogous to the question of assisted suicide.

FURTHER STUDY

Catechism of the Catholic Church, §§2276–2283.

Catholic Answers at Catholic.com

+ Jimmy Akin, "The Doctor-Assisted Suicide Debate," September 16, 2015.

+ Trent Horn, "On the So-Called 'Choice in Dying,'" October 10, 2014.

+ Tim Staples, "Death With Dignity?" October 17, 2015.

+ Fr. Frank Pavone, "What About the Right to Die?" October 1, 2005.

Wesley J. Smith, *Forced Exit: Euthanasia, Assisted Suicide, and the New Duty to Die* (New York: Encounter Books, 2006).

Austen Ivereigh, "Assisted Suicide," in *How to Defend the Faith without Raising Your Voice: Civil Responses to Catholic Hot-Button Issues* (Huntington, Indiana: Our Sunday Visitor Publishing Division, 2012), 58–70.

United States Conference of Catholic Bishops, "To Live Each Day With Dignity: A Statement on Physician-Assisted Suicide," June 16, 2011, available at usccb.org.

CONTRACEPTION

Why does the Church forbid the use of contraception?

Objection 1
The Scriptures do not forbid the use of contraceptives, so the Church should not forbid them either.

Objection 2
Marital intimacy is not only about procreation but also about uniting and deepening the love between spouses. By allowing sexual intimacy when there are good reasons to avoid pregnancy, contraception leads to improved marriages and family life.

Objection 3
By limiting the number of unwanted children, contraception reduces the number of abortions, which is a far greater evil than contraception.

Objection 4
Contraception has been essential to greater autonomy for women. It has given them freedom, prosperity, and control over their lives. Turning the clock back on women's rights is simply not an option.

Objection 5
Contraception contributes to public health by limiting the spread of disease. It also protects a woman for whom a pregnancy would be dangerous or even life-threatening.

Objection 6
Like contraception, Natural Family Planning obstructs the procreative dimension of sexual relations. It is essentially Catholic contraception. Church teaching is therefore inconsistent and should be rejected.

CATHOLIC TEACHING

+ **Marriage is a permanent relationship of love and service** created by God and entered into by the free consent of a man and a woman. It is both a natural bond and a Christian sacrament. It is ordered to the good of the couple and also to the common good because, **through marriage, children are conceived, and in family life, they are raised. Fertility is therefore a blessing from God** to which a married couple responds, as a fundamental consequence of their vocation, with generosity and faith. "Called to give life, spouses share in the creative power and fatherhood of God" (CCC §§2367).

+ **The natural end of each marital act is both procreative and unitive.** The constant teaching of the Church from the beginning (and of Protestant communions until 1930) has affirmed that **deliberately obstructing one of these primary ends of marriage is a violation of the natural law, diminishes the dignity of the marital bond, and is an offense against God** who wills to create children through human cooperation. In fact, we call human generation "procreation" rather than mere "reproduction" because there is a direct, creative act of God in the generation of each immortal human soul.

+ Many factors may influence a couple's decisions regarding responsible and generous parenthood. **A couple may choose to abstain from the marital act for discrete periods of time** if they believe, through prayer and reflection, that such is God's will. Nevertheless, this choice should be made only for serious reasons and for a limited period of time.

+ In his encyclical *Humanae Vitae*, **Pope Paul VI predicted grave consequences for ignoring the historic teaching on contraception**: infidelity, a lowering of sexual morality, loss of respect for women, and sexual exploitation.[1] These consequences have been tragically realized since the "contraceptive boom" in the 1950s.

REPLY

Reply to Objection 1: The Scriptures do not forbid contraceptives.
Early Jewish and Christian thinkers often cited the story of Onan, who

---

[1]   Pope Pius XII, Encyclical Letter On Human Life *Humanae Vitae*, July 25, 1968, §17.

"spilled his seed on the ground" (Gen 38:9), in their rejection of contraception. While some modern commentators object that God was simply angry with Onan for failing to produce a child with his dead brother's wife, it is clear from Deuteronomy 25:9–10 that penalty for this sin is public humiliation, not death as Onan's actions provoked. Some scholars also point out that New Testament injunctions against *pharmakeia*, or "sorcery" or "the use of drugs" (for instance, in Gal 5:20 and Rev 21:8), could refer to contraceptive potions. Catholics, however, do not rely only on explicit biblical injunctions to know the moral law. The Magisterium of the Church teaches and explains enduring moral truths in the new circumstances of every age, including our own, particularly as technological and cultural conditions change.

Reply to Objection 2: Contraception leads to stronger marriages and better family life.
While sexual relations can, of course, foster marital love even when a child is not conceived, it is never licit to deliberately obstruct the procreative end of sexual intimacy. The question at hand is whether contraception itself is wrong, not what presumed benefits might derive from it. Moreover, it is not at all certain that, compared to Natural Family Planning, contraception truly helps marriages or children. For instance, couples that use NFP have dramatically lower divorce rates, usually estimated at 1 to 5 percent. The growth in communication, personal discipline, and sacrifice reported by couples who use NFP strengthens marriages and families. In addition, NFP can promote a humbler view of children that more readily accepts them as gifts and blessings from God.

Reply to Objection 3: The use of contraception contributes to fewer abortions.
Contraception has conveyed a false sense of security that sexual relations can be free of consequences. The "sexual revolution" of the 1960s, which fueled an explosion of unwanted pregnancies and precipitated the intense demand for legalized abortion, was only made possible by contraception. When abortion was legalized in the United States, *after* the proliferation of contraception, the number of abortions more than doubled in the following two decades. Abortion has become, in effect, back-up contraception. Thus while contraception might prevent some abortions from taking place, on the whole it has caused many more. Indeed, today some forms of contraception are themselves abortifacients that prevent the implantation of newly-conceived embryos, further exposing the weakness of this objection.

Reply to Objection 4: Contraception empowers women to gain control over their reproductive lives.

In many respects women's lives have deteriorated dramatically since the 1960s. Young women no longer have any "excuse" to refuse sex. They are subjected to intense pressure to conform to promiscuous behavior, which is often emotionally devastating and exacerbates an image of women as sex-objects, reinforced by movies, television, and the internet. Single motherhood, a primary cause of poverty and social disenfranchisement, is far more widespread due to the more cavalier attitudes toward sex made possible by contraception. Finally, many studies reveal harmful side effects of the contraceptive pill including depression, infertility, decreased sex drive, increased risk of breast cancer, blood clots, and stroke. In 2005 the World Health Organization even declared hormonal contraception a Group 1 Carcinogen. Contraception is not exactly the blessing to women that it promised to be. Women's equality and freedom are important goods that should not be held hostage to contraception, which imposes more burdens than it lifts.

Reply to Objection 5: Contraception limits the spread of disease and protects women from life-threatening pregnancies.

Even if this were the case, it is never permissible to do evil that good may come of it. The question, then, is whether contraception is morally justified. Moreover, outside of marriage, the only definitive way to avoid sexually transmitted diseases is to abstain from sexual relations. Within marriage, when disease or dangerous pregnancies threaten, couples must seek a morally licit means to reduce or eliminate the risk. If no such means exists, then the couple must abstain from sexual relations until such means can be found. In no case should contraception, which is an offense against God and against marital love, be used simply in order to avoid undesired outcomes.

Reply to Objection 6: Natural Family Planning is "Catholic contraception."

Catholic couples are not required by divine law to engage in sexual relations at all times, and hence may choose, for a variety of reasons, when to engage in marital intercourse. Such periodic abstention, using the very cycle of fertility created by God, does not preclude an openness to God's will regarding children in any specific act or in the marriage as a whole. That is to say, limiting a natural power has not the same moral repercussions as subverting a natural power. An analogy can be made to eating: one should not subvert the natural faculty of eating by gorging oneself on pleasurable food and then vomiting it up in order to avoid the weight gain. On the other hand, while we should eat, we can always decide (as in a diet) to fast or to limit our intake of food. The former is analogous to contraception, the latter to NFP.

FURTHER STUDY

Catechism of the Catholic Church, §§2366–2372.

Catholic Answers at Catholic.com

- "What the Early Church Believed: Contraception and Sterilization," Tract, August 10, 2004.

- Karlo Broussard, "How Contraception Thwarts Love," July 25, 2018.

- Kenneth Howell, "What's Wrong with Contraception, Anyway?" July 1, 2005.

- Todd Aglialoro, "Contraception and Abortion: A Love Story," March 7, 2013.

- Stacy Trasancos, "Can Contraception Cause Abortions?" January 22, 2018.

- Laura Locke, "Contraception's Dark Fruits," March 1, 2012.

- Patrick Coffin, "How Is Natural Family Planning Different from Contraception?" July 29, 2019.

Janet Smith, "Contraception: Why Not?" in *Catholic Education Resource Center.* (Also available as a talk at janetsmith.org.)

Staff of Catholic Answers, "Birth Control," in *The Essential Catholic Survival Guide: Answers to Tough Questions About the Faith* (San Diego: Catholic Answers, 2005), 280–286.

Cormac Burke, "Married Love and Contraception," in *Catholic Controversies: Understanding Church Teachings and Events in History*, ed. Stephen Gabriel (Falls Church, Virginia: Moorings Press, 2010), 421–432.

Mary Eberstadt, "The Vindication of *Humanae Vitae*," in *Catholic Controversies: Understanding Church Teachings and Events in History*, ed. Stephen Gabriel (Falls Church, Virginia: Moorings Press, 2010), 433–449.

IN VITRO FERTILIZATION

Why does the Church prohibit in vitro fertilization?

Objection 1

There are many couples who earnestly desire children and have the means to provide a good home for them. In vitro fertilization (IVF) provides such couples with the possibility of having children and should not be prohibited.

Objection 2

There are many side benefits to IVF. For instance, since there are often more embryos created in the IVF process than are needed, doctors and parents can determine through prenatal testing which embryo is healthiest. This will reduce disease and genetic anomalies in babies. In addition, unused embryos created in the IVF process provide material (in the form of embryonic stem cells) for medical research, thus potentially yielding tremendous medical cures. Finally, extra embryos can make possible the production of biologically compatible organs for their living siblings, adding still further to the potential medical benefits of IVF.

Objection 3

In vitro fertilization would allow single persons or homosexual couples to have children, many of whom can offer loving and supportive homes.

Objection 4

IVF would allow parents to select the traits of their child—either by choosing an embryo with specific characteristics or by modifying the genetic material in the embryo—which would contribute to the happiness of the parents and happier homes for children.

CATHOLIC TEACHING

+ **Children, like all human beings, are made in the image and likeness of God and enjoy inalienable rights, including the right to life.** A child's value is not found in his or her productivity, genetic traits, or in satisfying a couple's desire to have a child. It does not depend upon the circumstance of the child being of a certain age—whether minutes or years—or whether the child is born or unborn.

+ **Fertility and children are gifts and blessings from God, not human rights.** In God's providence he entrusts children to the couples and at the time that he chooses.

+ **Even when a child is conceived or born in ways contrary to the moral law, his or her dignity remains undiminished.** This must be emphasized, especially when parents who have conceived children through IVF later realize the moral dimensions of their decision. A child is always a blessing from God, no matter how he or she came into being.

+ Infertility often causes deep anguish to married couples, and Christians must respond to this suffering with sincere compassion. Nevertheless, **infertility does not justify immoral behavior.**

+ **Every child has a natural right to be conceived in a way commensurate with his or her human dignity,** through an act of love by the father and mother. In vitro fertilization does not respect this basic right of each child. **The choice for surrogacy further complicates the morality of IVF** since every child has a right to be born of his or her own mother.

+ The Church has repeatedly defended the integrity of the sexual act as open to both conception (the procreative end) and to the love of the spouses (the unitive end). In the case of contraception, masturbation, and homosexual acts, for instance, the procreative end has been detached. **IVF, by contrast, seeks the power of procreation outside the union of love of the spouses. It turns procreation into a medical act rather than an embrace of love. It therefore diminishes the dignity of the marital act and of the spouses, and constitutes an offense against God.**

+ Moreover, **IVF generates embryos with the presumption that many of them will eventually be killed or left to die.** The Church teaches that "from the time that the ovum is fertilized, a new life is begun which is neither that of the father nor of the mother; it is rather the life of a new human being with his own growth."[1] It is always wrong to kill innocent human beings through either direct means or indirect neglect. This is not only an offense against the dignity and rights of those embryos, but it also contributes to an "abortion-mentality which has made this procedure possible" and "leads, whether one wants it or not, to man's domination over the life and death of his fellow human beings and can lead to a system of radical eugenics."[2]

+ **For couples struggling with infertility, the answer is not to be found in IVF.** The couple can seek methods of enhancing fertility that aim to restore their natural capacity to conceive children without changing the nature of the marital act or replacing it altogether. In the end, however, if God does not grant the couple children, they are encouraged to embrace that suffering with serenity, united to the sufferings of Our Lord, and to be confident that he will bring great good out of that trial. These couples are also encouraged to prayerfully consider adopting one or more children who otherwise might not enjoy the benefits of a loving home.

REPLY

Reply to Objection 1: In vitro fertilization gives sterile couples an opportunity to have children.
Though the desire to have children is itself a good and noble longing for a married couple, no one has a right to children. The question under consideration is whether IVF is a morally legitimate means to generate offspring since good ends do not justify immoral means. The desires of the couple, important as they are, do not make IVF morally good.

Reply to Objection 2: There are multiple medical benefits of surplus embryos.
The argument that surplus embryos can be put to medical use is a rather disturbing defense of IVF. Choosing the healthiest embryo (to

---

[1] Congregation for the Doctrine of the Faith, Instruction on Respect for Human Life in its Origin and on the Dignity of Procreation *Donum Vitae*, February 22, 1987, I.1.

[2] *Donum Vitae*, II.

reduce incidents of disease and genetic anomalies) while leaving the others to die, or destroying embryos to harvest their stem cells, or cultivating embryos to provide body parts to siblings are all examples of eugenics. It shows a callous disregard for the embryos simply because they are tiny. Embryos, in fact, are the most vulnerable and helpless human beings and deserve our protection more than anyone. It is always wrong to intentionally harm or destroy them.

Reply to Objection 3: In vitro fertilization offers single parents an option to have children.
If married parents do not have a natural right to children, still less do those who in principle cannot conceive children, such as single people and homosexual couples. In addition, just as a child has a right to be conceived by his or her own parents and born of his or her own mother, the norm and ideal for rearing a child is in the home of the mother and father. Exceptions to this, of course, are inevitable, as when a father or mother dies when their children are still young. Still, these exceptions should never be chosen as a matter of course or enshrined in law, particularly when the child would be raised in a morally harmful or confusing situation like that of a homosexual couple.

Reply to Objection 4: In vitro fertilization allows parents to select certain traits in their children.
Practicing IVF with the intention of selecting certain traits in children is an even greater moral offense. The trait-selection mentality goes beyond the dangerous eugenics path of embryo "reduction" for the sake of avoiding disease or providing stem cells; it is the ultimate trivialization of the blessing of children. Shopping for genetic traits stands in stark contrast to the attitude of grateful receptivity that should characterize parenthood. It leads to the commodification of children and treats them not as gifts from God but as products to be purchased as a lifestyle accessory. If IVF is wrong, using it for this purpose is doubly so.

FURTHER STUDY

Catechism of the Catholic Church, §§2373–2379.

Catholic Answers at Catholic.com

+ Dr. George Delgado, "Why is In Vitro Fertilization wrong?" November 19, 2018.

+ Todd Aglialoro, "The Hardest Teaching of Them All," September 4, 2014.

+ Stephanie Gray Connors, "In Vitro Fertilization," July 10, 2019.

+ Scott Richert, "The Brave New World of IVF," June 8, 2017.

John F. Doerfler, "*In Vitro* Fertilization and the Person," in *Catholic Controversies: Understanding Church Teachings and Events in History*, ed. Stephen Gabriel (Falls Church, Virginia: Moorings Press, 2010), 482–486.

John M. Haas, "Begotten Not Made: A Catholic View of Reproductive Technology" (Washington, D.C.: United States Conference of Catholic Bishops, 1998), available at usccb.org.

William May, *Marriage: The Rock on Which the Family is Built* (San Francisco: Ignatius Press, 2009).

ANIMAL RIGHTS

Do animals have a right to life?

Objection 1
Humans have a right to life because humans can experience pain. But most other animals experience pain as well. Thus killing these animals is also wrong.

Objection 2
Some claim that the right to life in humans is based on their capacity to act morally, to know right from wrong. Animals cannot act morally and so do not have a right to life. This argument fails, however, whether its assumption is true or not. If animals are *not* capable of moral action, then they are incapable of committing evil and hence are innocent, and it is always wrong to kill the innocent. If animals *are* capable of moral action, then like humans, they enjoy a right to life. In any case, this criteria for personal rights is flawed since even many humans, such as small children and the mentally handicapped, are incapable of moral action. Thus animals need not be moral agents in order to possess a right to life.

Objection 3
The arbitrary exercise of power over others is unjust. If killing and eating animals were essential to human survival, it might be argued that killing animals is justified. However, the examples of vegetarians and vegans show that humans do not need to eat other animals in order to survive. Thus by denying animals their right to life, humans are arbitrarily exercising lethal power over others.

Objection 4
St. Thomas Aquinas, following Aristotle, argued that all animals have souls. But it is precisely the presence of the soul that establishes the foundation of rights, including the right to life.

Objection 5
In Genesis, God calls the creation of animals "good." It is wrong to destroy what God has called good and hence animals enjoy a right to life given by God.

CATHOLIC TEACHING

+ **Human beings alone possesses a rational soul.** We have a capacity to think that rises above instinct and simple communication and problem-solving. This power of reason is known, for instance, by our capacity to know, love, and worship God, by our capacity to make free choices, to reason abstractly, to appreciate irony and humor, and to be creative. Rationality exists in every human soul even though its powers are not exercised at all times (e.g., in sleep) or in every individual (e.g., infants). In addition, the immateriality of the human soul can be known by reason, including the fact that it is not subject to decay after death.

+ **Human rationality and immortality are also known through revelation.** Scripture teaches that human beings alone are formed in the "image" and "likeness" of the Creator (Gen 1:26–27), signifying their freedom, reason, and will. Scripture affirms human immortality since God gave his only Son "that whoever believes in him should not perish but have eternal life" (John 3:16).

+ **The rational soul of human beings and our immortal destiny are the basis for our personal rights, including the right to life,** since we are "the only creature on earth that God has willed for its own sake" (CCC §356). These rights are not shared by other animals. Christ himself indicates our relative value to animals: "You are of more value than many sparrows" (Luke 12:7) and "of how much more value is man than a sheep" (Matt 12:12). In addition, Jesus ate animals such as fish and lamb.

+ God entrusts human beings with the stewardship of creation, commanding us to "fill the earth and subdue it" and giving us dominion over "every living thing that moves upon the earth" (Gen 1: 28). **In exercising their stewardship, men and women may use God's creation for their own sustenance and well-being.**

+ **As good stewards, human beings are also called to respect cre-**

ation (see CCC §2417). Animals "are God's creatures. He surrounds them with his providential care. By their mere existence they bless him and give him glory. Thus men owe them kindness" (CCC §2416). It is "contrary to human dignity to cause animals to suffer or die needlessly. It is likewise unworthy to spend money on them that should as a priority go to the relief of human misery" (CCC §2418).

REPLY

Reply to Objection 1: Animals can experience pain.
It is not the experience of pain that renders an action unjust; nor is it the capacity to feel pain that endows rights. If, for instance, an unconscious person is harmed physically, it is still morally wrong whether or not the victim feels pain; and on the other hand, surgery to heal a disease is morally praiseworthy even if it causes pain. Rather, actions are morally wrong when they are unjust, that is, when they fail to give others their due by intentionally withholding a good that belongs to them. Therefore the mere sensation of pain does not endow a creature with the right to life.

Reply to Objection 2: Animals need not be moral agents to have right to life.
The capacity to act as moral agents, knowing right and wrong, comes from our capacity to reason. Rationality exists, at least potentially, in all human beings and at all times, even when it is not being exercised or when it is impeded by age or disability. A person does not cease being rational because he or she is asleep, old, or disabled. It is precisely this rationality which does not exist in other animals and which underlies the human right to life. Furthermore, the "innocence" of animals is not that of moral goodness because animals can be neither good nor evil; it is simply the absence of moral capacity. This is why killing animals is not an instance of "killing the innocent."

Reply to Objection 3: Denying animal rights is unjust exercise of power.
Human beings should respect God's creation over which we have been placed as stewards. Our stewardship, however, is not based upon our relative power over animals but rather on our inherent superiority to animals. We are endowed with immortal souls and destined for eternal life. Our use of animals for our sustenance and well-being is, therefore, not a tyrannical abuse of power but a fitting exercise of

our authority as stewards. Moreover, if denying rights to animals is an abuse of power, then endowing animals with rights would oblige humans, as moral agents themselves, to defend animals whose "right to life" is endangered by other animals, rendering the argument absurd.

Still, there is some merit in this objection; as noted above, it is "contrary to human dignity to cause animals to suffer or die needlessly" (CCC §2418). Pitting dogs against each other for sport, for instance, while not violating any personal rights (for dogs have none), is nonetheless immoral on the part of the dog-fighter. It shows an unreasonable wish to see God's creation harmed, and it may stimulate cruel and immoral thoughts or behavior on the part of dog-owners and spectators.

Reply to Objection 4: St. Thomas Aquinas taught that animals have souls.
In line with ancient wisdom, St. Thomas Aquinas held that all living things are composed of a soul and a body. He classifies these souls according to vital functions, with each higher form encompassing the lower. Thus plants possess vegetative souls, animals possess sentient (feeling) souls, and human beings alone possess rational souls. It is this rational, immortal soul, imbuing human beings with freedom, intelligence, and will, that makes possible our pursuit of the good and endows us with rights and duties, including the right to life.

Reply to Objection 5: God called animals "good," and thus we should not kill them.
Animals, and in fact all creatures, are objectively good, and the virtuous person, as a good steward, will treat them well and in a reasonable way. As noted above, however, it does not follow that non-human animals have rational souls or personal rights, such as the right to life. Indeed, the argument that we should not kill animals because they are declared "good" by God would apply equally to plants, which renders the claim absurd since then human beings would have no means to sustain themselves.

FURTHER STUDY

Catechism of the Catholic Church, §§2415–2418.

Catholic Answers at Catholic.com

+ Matt Nelson, "Do You Know What Separates Man from the Animals?" March 23, 2017.

Mortimer Adler, *The Difference of Man and the Difference It Makes* (New York: Fordham University Press, 1993).

Steven Jensen, *The Human Person: A Beginner's Thomistic Psychology* (Washington, D.C.: The Catholic University of America Press, 2018).

CAPITAL PUNISHMENT

As noted earlier, the treatment on capital punishment takes a different format than the other questions in this book. In light of a recent change to the Catechism of the Catholic Church, the topic is presented as a defense of both sides of this prudential question. It is presumed that the Catechism change is not intended as a radical break from the ancient teaching of the Church and the Scriptures, and the matter is addressed accordingly.

Revision to the Catechism

The revised paragraph of the Catechism on capital punishment states, "Recourse to the death penalty on the part of legitimate authority, following a fair trial, was long considered . . . an acceptable, albeit extreme, means of safeguarding the common good." After observing "an increasing awareness that the dignity of the person is not lost even after the commission of very serious crimes" and modern developments of "more effective systems of detention" the Catechism goes on to say, "the Church teaches, in light of the Gospel, that 'the death penalty is inadmissible because it is an attack on the inviolability and dignity of the person'" (CCC §2267).

WHAT ARE THE ARGUMENTS IN FAVOR OF CAPITAL PUNISHMENT?

Continuity with Catholic teaching

Some theologians argue that even with the stronger Catechism statement, it is still possible for Catholics to hold that capital punishment is theoretically admissible, especially if otherwise it becomes impossible for a nation to safeguard the common good. The practice, after all, is allowed and even commanded by God in the Old Testament. The New Testament, though never explicitly approving of the death penalty, does not censure it either—and Jesus may implicitly endorse it (see Matt 15:4). Almost without exception the ancient Fathers and Church Doctors supported capital punishment. The Roman Catechism of the Council of Trent explicitly reaffirmed the teaching. Capital punishment was in the penal code of the Vatican City State until 1969. Thus while the stronger words in the Catechism should give pause to every Catholic who endorses capital punishment today, such a position may still be held given that the new paragraph should be read in continuity with the historical Catholic teaching.

Protection of the common good

Even with our modern jails, it may be possible for particularly dangerous criminals or crime syndicate leaders to bribe officials, to escape, or to oversee criminal, even murderous, activity from within jail. In these cases it may be morally licit or even necessary to employ capital punishment to safeguard the common good.

Justice

Capital punishment is a justified response to an assault on human life. Genesis 9:6 says that "Whoever sheds the blood of man, by man shall his blood be shed; for God made man in his own image." Retribution by the death penalty is not for motives of personal revenge but rather a recognition of the gravity of a crime that defaces the image of God in another person. It is the role of the nation to uphold the true value and dignity of human life, when necessary even (paradoxically) through capital punishment. Indeed lifelong imprisonment, the usual alternative to capital punishment, is also denying someone an important human right—liberty—though not as fundamental a right as life itself.

Rehabilitation

The death penalty excludes rehabilitation in the restricted sense, that is, the criminal being restored to society. On the other hand, "rehabilitation" can take on a deeper significance as an opportunity for repentance and conversion in preparation for death and judgment for those who cannot be reintegrated into society. In this light, capital punishment may—and, at least anecdotally, some evidence seems to support it—provide a greater motivation for repenting of grievous crimes by focusing the mind on the certitude and the proximity of one's death.

Deterrence

There seems little evidence that modern capital punishment has been a widespread deterrent to crime, especially without the public and horrifying spectacles of executions in the past. Indeed, since the number of executions is miniscule compared to the amount of violent crime in our society, it is difficult to see how it could be a deterrent under current conditions. Interestingly, though, for the one crime that does more regularly incur the death penalty—the killing of a police officer—there is evidence that it has, in fact, deterred the crime and saved the lives of policemen.

WHAT ARE THE ARGUMENTS AGAINST CAPITAL PUNISHMENT?

Viable options

Jesus does not explicitly condemn capital punishment. His teachings on forgiveness pertain to individual persons who have suffered injury, not to the legitimate demands of justice. Nevertheless, the tenor of Jesus' teachings is one of compassion and mercy, and it seems likely that—assuming a viable alternative is available—he would want Christians to avoid inflicting capital punishment. In fact, the Church teaches that today "there is an increasing awareness that the dignity of the person is not lost even after the commission of very serious crimes" and that "in the light of the Gospel . . . the death penalty is inadmissible because it is an attack on the inviolability and dignity of the person" (CCC §2267). Modern penal systems provide viable alternatives to capital punishment, and those alternatives should be employed, even in the most extreme cases, rather than having recourse to the death penalty.

Witness to life

Though there are important distinctions between capital punishment and crimes against life, these distinctions are not always perceived or understood by modern audiences. On a practical basis, then, opposing capital punishment enhances the persuasiveness of the Catholic defense of life by ruling out any, even false, charges of inconsistency. Furthermore, capital punishment—at least in the contemporary era—may unwittingly contribute to a culture that is hostile to innocent human life. Catholic support for it obscures the Church's opposition to evils such as abortion and doctor-assisted suicide.

Danger of innocent deaths

Even in countries where trials are fair and serious efforts are made to come to an accurate judgment, errors are made. Some of these errors are corrected by appellate courts. Other death-row convicts have been exonerated by later DNA evidence. The injustice of these false convictions is deeply aggravated when the innocent defendant is executed. Given that there are viable options for convicted offenders, it is therefore reasonable to choose the less permanent options and forgo capital punishment.

Rehabilitation

For criminals who can be rehabilitated into society, a lengthy prison term offers them an opportunity to repent and convert. The death penalty cuts this opportunity short.

Scandal

Capital punishment can cause scandal, in the true sense of the word, by leading others into sin. It can contribute to sinful thoughts of vengeance and lead to hatred by whetting an inordinate appetite for revenge rather than the fulfillment of true justice.

Secular morality

The Church's position on capital punishment presumes that states are agents of God. It is true that ancient Fathers defended capital punishment even when civil rulers were not Christian or even violently opposed to Christianity. Nevertheless, the argument for capital punishment loses some of its force when nations are governed by moral principles that seem to be more and more removed from their Christian roots.

Magisterial momentum

While the state, in principle, has the right to impose the death penalty for the commission of serious crimes, there are also many compelling arguments that lean in the other direction, and it is up to believers to make a judicious determination of their relative strengths. However, recent popes, as well as most bishops, have regularly taught that, in light of current circumstances, capital punishment does more harm than good. In light of this uncertainty, the more prudent option is to follow the more merciful option.

FURTHER STUDY

Catechism of the Catholic Church, §§2263–2267.

Catholic Answers at Catholic.com

- Trent Horn, "How Is Capital Punishment Different From Abortion and Euthanasia?" November 19, 2018.

- Jimmy Akin, "Understanding the Catechism Revision on the Death Penalty," August 8, 2018.

- Tim Staples, "The Church and Capital Punishment," May 29, 2015.

- Gerald Korson, "The Catholic Case for Capital Punishment," May 1, 2017.

- Trent Horn, "The Pope, the Death Penalty, and the Catechism," August 10, 2018.

E. Christian Brugger, *Capital Punishment and Roman Catholic Moral Tradition* (South Bend, Indiana: University of Notre Dame Press, 2004).

Avery Cardinal Dulles, "Catholicism and Capital Punishment," *First Things* 112 (April 2001): 30–35.

GENDER DYSPHORIA

*Why is transgenderism incompatible
with Church teaching?*

Objection 1
Gender is "who I really am," and biological sex refers to the bodily
organs I happen to have. Particular sex organs are not essential to a
person's humanity or dignity and can be modified through medical
procedures and other therapies.

Objection 2
Some people manifest an internal conflict between their biological
sex and their gender (gender dysphoria). If, in order to attain greater
inner peace, they choose to identify with an alternative gender, no
one has a right to tell them otherwise. We should respect the gender
choices of others.

Objection 3
Intersex people are born with sex characteristics that cannot be neatly
classified as either male or female. These individuals demonstrate
conclusively that gender is a fluid continuum. It is therefore not only
unjust but also unscientific to limit human genders to male and female.

Objection 4
Respecting transgender people is a major civil rights issue today.
Imposing binary gender theories on others leads to injustice, bigotry,
fear, and often violence against transgender persons.

Objection 5
Binary gender thinking contributes to outdated stereotypes of masculine and feminine expectations which stifle genuine human fulfillment.

CATHOLIC TEACHING

+ **Sexual identity refers to the human quality of being male or female.** We are comprised of both soul and body, both essential to who we are as human beings. Since the body is male or female down to our very DNA, our sexual identity is integral to who we are as human beings created in the "image" and "likeness" of God. Being male or female reflects "the power and tenderness of God, with equal dignity though in a different way" (CCC §2335).

+ **Part of a healthy, thriving human life includes accepting the particular corporal nature we are born with.** This means learning to love, care for, and develop our bodies. We are stewards, not owners, of our lives—both body and soul.

+ **Biological sex and gender are interdependent realities.** Sex refers to the physical quality of being male or female, starting with chromosomal differences. Gender, when it is not meant synonymously with sex, can refer to certain dispositions or traits characteristic of femininity or masculinity. It is derived primarily from one's biological sex and secondarily from cultural norms and personal choices. In the words of Pope Francis, "biological sex and the socio-cultural role of sex (gender) can be distinguished but not separated."[1]

+ **Detaching gender from biological sex reveals a dualistic anthropology.** The human person is a unity of body and soul. When this integration is lost—"dis-integrated"—then our self-identity becomes confused and conflicted. On the one hand, we see ourselves as slaves of the unchosen impulses and desires of our bodies. On the other hand, we see ourselves as possessing total self-dominion, able to modify and even create ourselves at will, including our bodies, as far as technology will allow. **The first error disregards our capacity for virtue to overcome bodily impulses. The second error disregards the "givenness" of our integrated human nature.**

+ Those who experience gender dysphoria experience a conflict between their biological sex and their perceived gender. **They**

---

[1] Pope Francis, Post-Synodal Apostolic Exhortation On Love in the Family *Amoris Laetitia*, March 19, 2016, §56.

always deserve our compassion and respect. It is not compassionate, however, to suggest that their psychological distress can be resolved by surrendering to a false identity. True compassion will encourage and help each person to accept and embrace his or her own body, a process that may be difficult and will usually include both spiritual and psychological assistance.

REPLY

Reply to Objection 1: "Gender is who I really am."
Biological sex begins in a specific genotype (XX or XY chromosome) that is embedded in every cell in the body. This cannot be changed. A person's phenotype, including reproductive organs, can sometimes be modified hormonally or surgically. Gender is closely related to biological sex since it involves our self-understanding as objectively male or female, though it is influenced by social norms of masculinity and femininity. Thus, while both sex and gender are susceptible to some external influence, neither is malleable, and both find their origins in the actual physical body. The sharp separation of sex and gender suggested by the objection is not an accurate picture of reality.

Reply to Objection 2: We've no right to restrict others' gender choices.
We should indeed respect the choices of others. We need not, however, always agree with them. Indeed, when someone's personal choices are harmful and based on flawed assumptions, we have a duty in charity and justice to disagree. In addition, the use of limited medical resources for morally-problematic hormonal therapies and sex "reassignment" surgeries is a question with important repercussions for the common good.

Reply to Objection 3: Intersex conditions show that gender is fluid.
Some intersex conditions such as Klinefelter syndrome and Turner's syndrome reflect a deviation from the normal genotypes XX and XY, while others cause a deviation between the genotype and the normal development of sexual organs. These disorders which result in ambiguous sexual characteristics call for deep compassion and individual treatments. Sometimes, for example, hormonal or surgical interventions can help approximate the sexual organs proper to one's biological sex. Intersex disorders, however, are not evidence for a spectrum of genders. In fact, the very word "intersex"—"between the sexes"—suggests the essentially binary character of human sexuality. Exceptions do not disprove a norm; they emphasize it. Gender dysphoria is very

different from intersex disorders. It is not a biological deviation, either in a person's genotype or phenotype, but rather the psychological distress caused by discomfort with one's sexual identity. It is often based on physical or sexual abuse or trauma. It should be treated with the same charity, and the same clarity, with which other distorted self-perceptions (such as body dysmorphic disorder or anorexia) are treated.

Reply to Objection 4: Imposing binary gender theories is a violation of civil rights.
Civil rights are an expression of human justice, which in turn is based upon the truth of the human person. Persons with gender dysphoria are entitled to full and equal treatment before the law. However, gender dysphoria is itself not a civil rights issue since it is based upon a false notion of the human person. Some activists, for instance, wish to eliminate male/female distinctions in public bathrooms and invoke the notorious Jim Crow laws that separated bathrooms along racial lines. Racial segregation, however, is unjust precisely because it is based on a human distinction (skin color) that is inconsequential to the use of bathrooms; whereas the reality of sexual difference is a human distinction that is entirely consequential to the use of bathrooms. The same applies to sports teams, locker rooms, the use of pronouns, and other similar "civil rights" claims. Respecting sexual difference, then, is not "imposing binary gender theories" on anyone but rather acknowledging the simple reality of the human condition.

Reply to Objection 5: Binary gender theories perpetuate harmful gender stereotypes.
It is true that in some cultures gender stereotypes have restricted the possibilities for human fulfillment for both men and women. The proper response, however, is not to reject all sexual difference in favor of a grim and monotonous androgyny. Nor is it, as in the case of transgender activism, to recast gender as changeable and idiosyncratic. We overcome rigid gender expectations by recognizing and valuing the characteristics proper to each sex while acknowledging diverse ways to be masculine and feminine. Human beings are not entirely pre-determined by biology since our free will can give different expressions to our sexual identities; nor are we unmoored from our bodies and left to fashion our own self-expression without any physical foundation.

FURTHER STUDY

Catechism of the Catholic Church, §§369–372, 2331–2336.

Catholic Answers at Catholic.com

- Trent Horn, "Five Questions for Supporters of Gender Transitioning," June 4, 2015.

- Trent Horn, "Two 'Transgender Traps' to Avoid," June 25, 2019.

- Fr. Dwight Longenecker, "Gender Confusion: The Unforeseen Offspring of Contraception," June 10, 2018.

- Matt Fradd, "The Science of Sex Differences," Matt Fradd, August 27, 2013.

- Todd Aglialoro, "Our Genders, Ourselves," June 12, 2013.

- Trent Horn, "Should Catholic Hospitals Offer Sex-Change Operations?" February 27, 2019.

Ryan T. Anderson, *When Harry Became Sally: Responding to the Transgender Moment* (New York: Encounter Books, 2018).

Dr. Ana Samuel, *Sex, Gender and Identity* (video available on YouTube), CanaVox, September 30, 2020.

Joseph Blackholm, *College Kids Say the Darndest Things: On Identity* (video available at familypolicyalliance.com), Family Policy Institute of Washington, April 13, 2016.

Sex Change Regret, www.sexchangeregret.com.

PORNOGRAPHY

Why is pornography a serious sin?

Objection 1
Viewing pornography is a private act that hurts nobody. Since it does no harm, it cannot be a sin.

Objection 2
The Church's prohibition against pornography reflects an obsession with sexual sins. Yet the Church itself teaches that the human body and sex are good. Its fixation on pornography is an inconsistent and arbitrary imposition of puritanical beliefs by celibate priests.

Objection 3
Pornography (especially when accompanied by masturbation) tempers the sexual drive, especially in men, which prevents worse sins, such as marital infidelity and fornication. In such cases, pornography can be morally licit or even praiseworthy.

Objection 4
Pornography is a way for women to be empowered. It offers well-paid, flexible, independent, and creative work. The prohibition against pornography is an example of ecclesiastical patriarchy curtailing the opportunities for ambitious women to succeed.

Objection 5
Pornography is a far less serious matter than sins such as adultery. Equating it to these more serious sins is an extreme exaggeration. If pornography is sinful, it certainly is not seriously so.

CATHOLIC TEACHING

+ **The human body, male or female, is integral to being made in the "image and likeness" of God** (Gen 1:26). It gives physical expression to the movements of our soul, including bonds of communion with others. God assuming a human body in the Incarnation dignifies the body still further. St. Paul even calls the human body a tabernacle of God when he writes to the Corinthians, "Do you not know that your body is a temple of the Holy Spirit within you?" (1 Cor 6:19).

+ **The dignity of the human body finds a powerful expression in the marital act.** Sexual union within marriage expresses a total and mutual self-gift, which is "a way of imitating in the flesh the Creator's generosity and fecundity" (CCC §2335). It is a reminder that a man and a woman, precisely through their bodily differences, dramatically reveal the love and fruitfulness of God.

+ **Pornography, by contrast, is the deliberate exploitation of human sexuality in order to gratify the carnal appetite.** It does "grave injury to the dignity of its participants (actors, vendors, the public), since each one becomes an object of base pleasure and illicit profit for others. It immerses all who are involved in the illusion of a fantasy world. It is a grave offense" (CCC §2354). As Jesus says, restating the Sixth Commandment, "You have heard that it was said, 'You shall not commit adultery.' But I say to you that every one who looks at a woman lustfully has already committed adultery with her in his heart" (Matt 5:27–28).

+ The sinfulness of pornography is many-layered:

    + Pornography is an **offense against charity** since it objectifies and demeans the models or actors involved in it.

    + Pornography is an **offense against justice**, particularly when it occurs in the context of marriage, since it is a form of marital infidelity.

    + Pornography **contributes to a self-absorbed narcissism** in which a person turns inward, focusing on his or her own self-gratification rather than the needs of others.

+ Pornography **fosters other sins, especially that of mastur-bation,** which is contrary to the purpose of the sexual faculty and is an "intrinsically and gravely disordered action" (CCC §2352).

+ Using pornography **contributes materially to a corrupt industry** steeped in the exploitation of adults and children, physical and sexual abuse, chemical addictions, and human trafficking.

+ Pornography is a **highly addictive drug** that enflames the desire for more and more perverse outlets for sexual satisfaction.

+ **Like all forms of lust, pornography is a kind of slavery.** Freedom can be found only in the virtue of chastity. Chastity means self-mastery, the successful integration of human sexuality, and is a source of immeasurable joy. "The alternative is clear," the Catechism states, "either man governs his passions and finds peace, or he lets himself be dominated by them and becomes unhappy" (CCC §2339). **It is chastity which enables us, whatever our state in life, to freely give ourselves to others in love.**

+ **The grace of God is a powerful aid to anyone who wishes to experience the freedom promised by Jesus.** "For freedom," St. Paul writes to the Galatians, "Christ has set us free" (Gal 5:1). The graces of repentance, forgiveness, and fortitude in the spiritual battle are never lacking to anyone who sincerely asks for them.

REPLY

Reply to Objection 1: Pornography does no harm.
There are many sins which seem to harm only the sinner (many interior acts of anger, for instance, or envy, or sloth) and yet are still immoral. Pornography, the use of another human being for one's sexual pleasure, would therefore still be a sin even were it harmful only to the sinner. However, it is definitely *not* harmful only to the sinner. Casualties of pornography include the human actors, whose dignity is compromised by being treated as objects of sexual gratification. They are, in fact, often victims themselves of manipulation, addictions, and sex trafficking—and, not infrequently, are minors, undocumented immi-

grants, or other vulnerable people. Marriages and families are further casualties of pornography. Pornographic infidelity (for what else is it?) devastates spouses, shatters trust, and often contributes to divorce. Finally, children are casualties of pornography; they are being introduced to pornography at an increasingly young age and are often traumatized, confused, and set upon a road that leads later to addictive and self-destructive behavior. The pretense that pornography does no harm is manifestly false.

Reply to Objection 2: The Church is obsessed with sexual sins.
The Church teaches that the human body and sex are good, and for that very reason she insists that both be treated with respect and even reverence. Naming sexual sins does not arise from a prudish desire to diminish sexual pleasure. It arises from a desire to protect the authentic goodness and nobility of sex. Indeed, the fact that these moral teachings are so prominent today is due not to the Church's obsession with sex but rather to the *world's* obsession with sex following the so-called "sexual revolution."

Reply to Objection 3: Pornography can prevent worse sexual sins.
We should never try to escape one sin by committing another. Sexual sin is no exception. Adultery and fornication are avoided not by viewing pornography and masturbating but by growing in the freedom and self-mastery of holy purity. Blunting the sexual drive by indulging in "private" sins is no replacement for chastity. Indeed, it often fosters sexual addictions that encourage addicts to act out sexually in more and more destructive ways.

Reply to Objection 4: Pornography is a means of empowering women.
Pornography does not promote the dignity of the woman. It degrades the beauty of her body and obscures the nobility of her soul. The problem with pornography, as some have said, is not that it shows too much of the person but that it shows too little. Women should not settle for tenuous social or material gains at the expense of their personal dignity. They have a right to be treated with the respect and honor that is due to every person without having to make such compromises.

Reply to Objection 5: Pornography is not a serious sin.
Objectifying another person for sexual pleasure is not a light matter. In some ways it is even more serious than "in person" sins, such as fornication, since pornography utterly abstracts a person from his or

her humanity, intellectually de-humanizing that person. When pornography is accompanied by masturbation, moreover, its sinfulness is amplified even further.

Of course, the Church always stipulates—and does so explicitly in the Catechism's section on these matters—that the seriousness of such sins can be diminished by a lack of adequate understanding or intentionality. Such factors include "affective immaturity, force of acquired habit, conditions of anxiety, or other psychological or social factors that can lessen, if not even reduce to a minimum, moral culpability" (CCC §2352).

FURTHER STUDY

Catechism of the Catholic Church, §§2337–2356.

Catholic Answers at Catholic.com

+ Matt Fradd, "Three Things You Need to Know About Pornography," February 7, 2013.

+ Devin Rose, "The Widely Known Secret of Pornography," December 8, 2015.

+ Matt Fradd, "Pornography Is Destroying Marriages," January 1, 2016.

Matt Fradd, *The Porn Myth: Exposing the Reality Behind the Fantasy of Pornography* (San Francisco: Ignatius Press, 2017).

United States Conference of Catholic Bishops, "Create in Me a Clean Heart" (Washington, D.C.: United States Conference of Catholic Bishops, 2015), available at usccb.org.

SAME-SEX ATTRACTIONS

Why does the Church teach that same-sex attractions are disordered?

Objection 1
Men and women with homosexual inclinations are born with their attractions. Since God is not the originator of anything disordered, it is not right to call these individuals disordered.

Objection 2
Even if homosexual behavior is judged to be immoral, sexual attractions are simply natural urges and not freely chosen. Thus, these attractions cannot themselves be disordered.

Objection 3
By teaching that same-sex attractions are disordered, the Church is effectively telling homosexual persons that they should repress their sexual feelings, which leads to self-destructive and often sinful behavior.

Objection 4
Same-sex unions are often more stable and loving than many heterosexual unions. This would not be the case were same-sex attractions disordered.

Objection 5
The Church's teaching that same-sex attractions are disordered contributes to injustices perpetrated against homosexual persons, including discrimination, bigotry, and even violence.

Objection 6
Nowhere in the Bible does it state that same-sex attractions are disordered.

CATHOLIC TEACHING

+ **The Church teaches that all human beings are called to holiness.** In seeking to grow in virtue, individuals with same-sex attraction are to struggle against the same concupiscence common to all human beings since the fall of Adam and Eve.

+ **Sexual activity has as its purpose not only the marital union but also the procreation of children,** which depends on and follows from the complementarity of the spouses. The natural bond of marriage—raised by Jesus to the level of a sacrament—is the proper environment for sexual union since children have a right to be raised in a family by parents who are in an exclusive, permanent, and faithful marital bond. Sexual activity outside of marriage is therefore sinful. Sexual sins are not the most serious sins—which are those stemming from pride—but arguably they are the most dangerous since they are probably the grave sins most commonly committed.

+ **Sinful desires lead to personal sin only when a person acts upon them,** either through external action or by engaging in fantasies which foster the desire. People tempted by improper desires, including homosexual temptations, do not sin unless they act on them.

+ Sexual urges for members of the *opposite* sex must be resisted when they are directed at anyone but one's spouse. At the same time, **such urges are not themselves intrinsically disordered since they *can* lead to a rightly ordered use of sexual activity in marriage.** Nevertheless, acting on these urges outside of marriage is gravely immoral.

+ Sexual urges for members of the *same* sex, however, are **"objectively disordered" (CCC §2358) since they can never lead to a rightly ordered use of sexual activity, and since they do not proceed from the complementarity of the sexes.** Since succumbing to those urges would always lead to sinful behavior, the urges themselves are disordered.

+ **Persons with same-sex attraction are called, like others, to live chastity.** "By the virtues of self-mastery that teach them inner freedom," the Catechism states, "at times by the support of disinterested friendship, by prayer and sacramental grace, they can and should gradually and resolutely approach Christian perfection" (CCC §2359). Such a struggle for chastity in homosexual persons can lead to great virtue and sanctity.

REPLY

Reply to Objection 1: People born with same-sex attractions should not be called disordered.

Those who struggle with same-sex attraction are, like all human beings, made in the image and likeness of God and certainly are not disordered, though same-sex attractions are. The effects of fallen human nature weigh on us all. While the Church says that the "psychological genesis" of homosexuality "remains largely unexplained" (CCC §2357), even if a genetic predisposition to homosexuality were to be demonstrated, it would not alter the teaching on homosexual attractions. If some are born with a genetic disposition to alcoholism, for instance, it would not justify the intemperate use of alcohol. Since homosexual activity is itself wrong, the same-sex attractions ordered to that activity cannot be ordered to the true good; and hence are themselves disordered.

Reply to Objection 2: Homosexual attractions are natural urges and thus cannot be immoral.

The Church teaches that the attractions, when they are not willed or fostered, are not themselves immoral (see CCC §1767). In fact, they are usually not chosen or desired by those who have them. These attractions, however, are disordered in that they cannot be directed to the person's authentic good. The Catechism states that "this inclination, which is objectively disordered, constitutes for most of them a trial. . . . These persons are called to fulfill God's will in their lives and, if they are Christians, to unite to the sacrifice of the Lord's Cross the difficulties they may encounter from their condition" (CCC §2358).

Reply to Objection 3: The Church's teaching leads to repressive and destructive behavior.

Everyone has feelings and urges that must not be acted on; it is inherent in the struggle for all virtue. The struggle for chastity is no different, and everyone (whatever their sexual attractions) must resist urges that are not ordered to their authentic good. Such resistance, when undertaken with affective maturity and freedom, does not lead to unhealthy emotional repression. The empirical data from the sexually permissive cultures, in fact, demonstrates the reverse in the case of homosexual persons. Studies consistently show that their widespread and tragically self-destructive behavior remains high even in the most liberal societies. Such behavior, in other words, is not a function of social stigma and sexual repression. These individuals need and deserve our compassion and the liberating truth of the Gospel, not mere affirmation of their sexual choices.

Reply to Objection 4: Many same-sex marriages are more stable than heterosexual marriages.
The fact that some same-sex unions are said to be more stable and loving than heterosexual unions does not make homosexual behavior (or the attractions that lead to it) praiseworthy. Stability and emotional affection can be found in other illicit unions too—in some adulterous relationships for instance—which are not thereby rendered morally good or the sexual attractions rightly ordered.

Reply to Objection 5: The Church's teaching contributes to bigotry and injustice.
The Church's teaching on same-sex attractions (and behavior) does not justify injustice in any form. The Catechism states that persons with homosexual tendencies "must be accepted with respect, compassion, and sensitivity. Every sign of unjust discrimination in their regard should be avoided" (CCC §2358). At the same time, shutting down rational conversation by lobbing charges of "homophobia" at anyone who holds to the Church's teachings is itself an injustice against those who embrace those doctrines in good faith.

Reply to Objection 6: The notion that same-sex attractions are disordered is nowhere found in the Bible.
The Bible teaches that same-sex attractions are disordered through its clear teaching that all homosexual behavior is immoral. St. Paul teaches that some homosexual desires emerge from a refusal to worship God: "Their women exchanged natural relations for unnatural, and the men likewise gave up natural relations with women and were consumed with passion for one another. . . . And since they did not see fit to acknowledge God, God gave them up to a base mind and to improper conduct" (Rom 1:26–28). St. Paul includes homosexual behavior in the list of sins that will deprive someone of heaven (see 1 Cor 6:9–10). These and other scriptural references demonstrate the clear teaching about all homosexual behavior, and hence the logical corollary about the disorder of homosexual attractions. They also remind us how important it is that Catholics continue to explain the Church's teaching on homosexual attractions and behavior, no matter how counter-cultural it is, since the good of many souls is at stake.

FURTHER STUDY

Catechism of the Catholic Church, §§2357–2359.

Catholic Answers at Catholic.com

+ "Homosexuality," Tract, August 10, 2004.

+ "What the Early Church Believed: Homosexuality," Tract, August 10, 2004.

+ Trent Horn, "The Bible on Homosexual Behavior," May 1, 2015.

+ Trent Horn, "'God Made Me Gay,'" April 11, 2019.

+ Trent Horn, "Homosexuality and the Catholic Church with Fr. Paul Check," (2 parts) August 28, 2018.

+ Fr. Philip Bochanski, "Same-Sex Attraction," July 1, 2019.

John Harvey, *Homosexuality and the Catholic Church: Clear Answers to Difficult Questions* (West Chester, PA: Ascension Press, 2007).

Living the Truth in Love: Pastoral Approaches to Same-Sex Attraction, eds. Janet E. Smith and Fr. Paul Check (San Francisco: Ignatius Press, 2015).

Patrick Madrid, "Homosexuality," in *Does the Bible Really Say That?: Discovering Catholic Teaching in Scripture* (Cincinnati: Servant, 2006), 33–35.

Austen Ivereigh, "Homosexuality and Contraception," in *How to Defend the Faith without Raising Your Voice: Civil Responses to Catholic Hot-Button Issues* (Huntington, Indiana: Our Sunday Visitor Publishing Division, 2012), 28–42.

Courage International, *Desire of the Everlasting Hills* (documentary video available on YouTube).

Staff of Catholic Answers, "Homosexuality," in *The Essential Catholic Survival Guide: Answers to Tough Questions About the Faith* (San Diego: Catholic Answers, 2005), 287–294.

Janet E. Smith, "Homosexuality," in *Catholic Controversies: Understanding Church Teachings and Events in History*, ed. Stephen Gabriel (Falls Church, Virginia: Moorings Press, 2010), 499–505.

SAME-SEX "MARRIAGE"

Should the state recognize same-sex marriages?

Objection 1
Marriage is the loving union of persons who pledge permanence, exclusivity, and fidelity and who raise and support any dependents they have. Two men or two women clearly can form such a union and therefore can be married.

Objection 2
Forbidding a same-sex couple to marry is to discriminate on the basis of sexual attractions, analogous to a prohibition on interracial marriage. Such discrimination and bigotry are clearly unjust.

Objection 3
It is said that sexual intercourse within marriage ought to be both procreative and unitive. But not all marital relations are procreative. Some couples are naturally infertile, for instance, or become so when a woman is past child-bearing age. Other couples choose infertility through contraception or sterilization. None of these cases, however, renders a couple incapable of marriage. Therefore, two men or two women can be married despite being infertile.

Objection 4
Many same-sex couples would provide a better home to adopted children than the homes of heterosexual couples or single parents. Thus they should be allowed to marry.

Objection 5
There is no harm in allowing same-sex couples to consider their relationships as marriages. In fact, allowing more loving couples to marry would strengthen a marriage culture. Therefore the state should recognize same-sex marriages.

Objection 6
Even if the Catholic Church is correct in its teaching on marriage, the state should not draw from religious teaching in crafting public policy, including laws pertaining to marriage.

CATHOLIC TEACHING

+ **Marriage alone is a complete union of persons.** Only the marital act shared between a man and a woman is comprehensive in that it unites them not only at an emotional, mental, and spiritual level (as indeed do many friendships) but at the bodily level by uniting in a shared procreative end. "The vocation to marriage is written in the very nature of man and woman as they came from the hand of the Creator" (CCC §1603). It is a mutual love which "becomes an image of the absolute and unfailing love with which God loves man. . . . And this love which God blesses is intended to be fruitful" (CCC §1604).

+ **This complete union is ordered to the good of the spouses and the generation and raising of children.** The only sexual act that can be fertile is male-female intercourse. This is why the possibility of procreating and raising children is essential to the marital relationship. It sets marriage apart from other types of friendships.

+ **As a human institution, marriage exists to bind parents to each other and to their children in a community of love, which is the family.** Friendship is neither necessarily permanent nor exclusive; only in marriage does the shared spousal commitment of child-bearing and rearing demand a permanent, monogamous, and faithful union of mothers and fathers, by whose love children will grow into flourishing adults. **We protect marriage in order to protect children.** Society depends for its vigor on healthy families and hence healthy marriages, and the state therefore has a compelling interest to protect marriage.

REPLY

Reply to Objection 1: Marriage is a union of love. It need not be heterosexual.

Marriage is not simply a union of love, which could describe almost any close friendship. What makes marriage unique is its capacity to be procreative, and this requires a man and a woman.

Reply to Objection 2: Forbidding homosexual marriages is unjust discrimination.

Justice means giving to each person his or her due. It includes the notion of fairness, applying standards evenly. Laws against interracial marriage are unfair because they call for unequal treatment of the same thing: people of different races are equally capable of entering into marriage. Two men, however, are not capable of entering into a genuine marriage because their union can never be procreative. This is why it is not unjust to refuse recognition of same-sex "marriages."

Reply to Objection 3: Since infertile couples can engage in sexual relations licitly, so can homosexual couples.

When a man and a woman unite in sexual relations, they are engaging in the *kind* of act that can generate a child. In any particular sexual act, of course, conception may or may not occur. It is a function of many factors. Nevertheless, the presence or absence of those factors does not change the fact that the marital act, in principle, can lead to conception. Sterility in these cases is circumstantial, even if it is due to a permanent medical condition or the age of the couple. Sterility in homosexual acts, on the other hand, is intrinsic to the act itself. The moral assessment of the two situations are, therefore, quite different.

Reply to Objection 4: Many homosexual couples would provide a better home for children than many heterosexual couples.

There may well be living arrangements which, in particular cases, are better for children than the home of their natural parents, especially when the home is violent or otherwise dysfunctional. The question is what family structure is in the best interest of children and society as a whole, and hence what should be normative and fostered through law and custom. The debate about same-sex "marriage" normally hinges on the desires of adults, and the best interests of children are often forgotten. But if children cannot be raised by their own mother and father, for whatever reason, we should endeavor to provide them with loving homes where they can still experience the love of a mother and a father. We should not relegate them, by law, to homes where they are deprived of it.

Reply to Objection 5: Homosexual marriage harms nobody and, in fact, fosters a marriage culture.
When a nation defines marriage as a sexual relationship between two men or two women, it obscures marriage's intrinsic ordering to children. This, in turn, diminishes our cultural understanding of marriage and weakens social support for those bearing the burden of raising the next generation. Far from strengthening the marriage culture, same-sex "marriage" weakens our appreciation for marriage as the basic building-block of society.

There are other ways that same-sex "marriage" has negative repercussions. First, when marriage is unmoored from its ordering to children, there is nothing to prevent other sexual and polyamorous relationships from being defined as marriage, further eroding the cultural underpinnings of marriage. This process has already begun in countries that have instituted same-sex "marriage." Second, as history has already demonstrated, redefining marriage so dramatically—and the governmental expansion of power that it depends upon—leads almost inevitably to coercive cultural and state-sponsored attempts at "re-education" and various impingements on religious and personal liberties. That process, too, has already begun. Third, legally permitting same-sex couples to consider their relationships as true marriages encourages them to pursue destructive and sinful sexual behavior. For all these reasons, it is false to claim that same-sex "marriage" does no harm.

Reply to Objection 6: The state should not guide marriage policy by religious tenets.
The arguments advanced in this chapter are drawn almost entirely from reason alone, not revelation. Many philosophical, legal, and historical traditions—some of which predate Christianity—recognize marriage as a distinct kind of relationship ordered to procreation and to the family as the fundamental component of society. The state does not need Christian revelation to perceive its dependence on healthy and fruitful marriages.

FURTHER STUDY

Catechism of the Catholic Church, §§1602–1617, 1625.

Catholic Answers at Catholic.com

- ✦ Todd Aglialoro, "Four Ways that Same-Sex Marriage Will Affect You," July 10, 2013.

- ✦ Trent Horn, "Same-Sex Marriage: Our Agreements Solve Our Disagreement," February 22, 2013.

Sherif Gergis, Robert George, and Ryan T. Anderson, *What is Marriage?: Man and Woman: A Defense* (New York: Encounter Books, 2012).

Patrick Lee, "Why Marriage is Inherently Heterosexual," in *Catholic Controversies: Understanding Church Teachings and Events in History,* ed. Stephen Gabriel (Falls Church, Virginia: Moorings Press, 2010), 506–510.

Austen Ivereigh, "Keep Marriage Conjugal," in *How to Defend the Faith without Raising Your Voice: Civil Responses to Catholic Hot-Button Issues* (Huntington, Indiana: Our Sunday Visitor Publishing Division, 2012), 122–137.

ACKNOWLEDGEMENTS

Above all I would like to thank the seminarians of St. John Paul II Seminary in Washington, D.C., who for the last ten years have engaged in these important discussions with me and who helped to refine the apologetics sheets from which many of these chapters were derived.

I would also like to thank Dr. John Grabowski, Fr. Daniel Hanley, Fr. Christian Huebner, Fr. Daniel Lorimer, Fr. David Pignato, Fr. Paul Scalia, Fr. Christopher Seith, and Fr. Gary Selin for reviewing portions of the manuscript to ensure doctrinal fidelity, as well as Fr. Conrad Murphy, Joseph McHenry, Robert Paulus, and Charles and Susan Griffin for helping to make it more readable.

Finally, I would like to thank the excellent staff at Emmaus Road, with whom it is always a joy to work. I am grateful to the editors of this book, Caroline Rock and Julia Snyder, as well as Emily Demary who did the design work. A special word of gratitude goes out to Melissa Girard who supervised the whole process with her characteristic professionalism and patience.